Presidents and Scandals

Other Books in the History Makers Series:

*History*MAKERS

Presidents and Scandals

By Russell Roberts

Lucent Books
P.O. Box 289011, San Diego, CA 92198-9011

Library of Congress Cataloging-in-Publication Data

Roberts, Russell, 1953–
Presidents and scandals / by Russell Roberts.
    p. cm. — (History makers)
Includes bibliographical references and index.
ISBN 1-56006-642-3 (alk. paper)
1. Presidents—United States—History—Juvenile literature. 2. Scandals—
United States—History—Juvenile literature. 3. Political corruption—United
States—History—Juvenile literature. 4. Presidents—United States—Biography—
Juvenile literature. [1. Presidents. 2. Political corruption.] I. Title. II. Series.
E176.1. R62 2001
973'.09'9—dc21
                                                    00-010224

CONTENTS

FOREWORD

The literary form most often referred to as "multiple biography" was perfected in the first century A.D. by Plutarch, a perceptive and talented moralist and historian who hailed from the small town of Chaeronea in central Greece. His most famous work, *Parallel Lives*, consists of a long series of biographies of noteworthy ancient Greek and Roman statesmen and military leaders. Frequently, Plutarch compares a famous Greek to a famous Roman, pointing out similarities in personality and achievements. These expertly constructed and very readable tracts provided later historians and others, including playwrights like Shakespeare, with priceless information about prominent ancient personages and also inspired new generations of writers to tackle the multiple biography genre.

The Lucent History Makers series proudly carries on the venerable tradition handed down from Plutarch. Each volume in the series consists of a set of five to eight biographies of important and influential historical figures who were linked together by a common factor. In *Rulers of Ancient Rome*, for example, all the figures were generals, consuls, or emperors of either the Roman Republic or Empire; while the subjects of *Fighters Against American Slavery*, though they lived in different places and times, all shared the same goal, namely the eradication of human servitude. Mindful that politicians and military leaders are not (and never have been) the only people who shape the course of history, the editors of the series have also included representatives from a wide range of endeavors, including scientists, artists, writers, philosophers, religious leaders, and sports figures.

Each book is intended to give a range of figures—some well known, others less known; some who made a great impact on history, others who made only a small impact. For instance, by making Columbus's initial voyage possible, Spain's Queen Isabella I, featured in *Women Leaders of Nations*, helped to open up the New World to exploration and exploitation by the European powers. Unarguably, therefore, she made a major contribution to a series of events that had momentous consequences for the entire world. By contrast, Catherine II, the eighteenth-century Russian queen, and Golda Meir, the modern Israeli prime minister, did not play roles of global impact; however, their policies and actions significantly influenced the historical development of both their own countries and their regional neighbors. Regardless of their relative importance in the greater historical scheme, all of the figures chronicled in the History Makers series made contributions to posterity; and their public achievements, as well as what is known about their private lives, are presented and evaluated in light of the most recent scholarship.

In addition, each volume in the series is documented and substantiated by a wide array of primary and secondary source quotations. The primary source quotes enliven the text by presenting eyewitness views of the times and culture in which each history maker lived; while the secondary source quotes, taken from the works of respected modern scholars, offer expert elaboration and/ or critical commentary. Each quote is footnoted, demonstrating to the reader exactly where biographers find their information. The footnotes also provide the reader with the means of conducting additional research. Finally, to further guide and illuminate readers, each volume in the series features photographs, two bibliographies, and a comprehensive index.

The History Makers series provides both students engaged in research and more casual readers with informative, enlightening, and entertaining overviews of individuals from a variety of circumstances, professions, and backgrounds. No doubt all of them, whether loved or hated, benevolent or cruel, constructive or destructive, will remain endlessly fascinating to each new generation seeking to identify the forces that shaped their world.

The Legacy of Power

Scandal has touched almost every president in the history of the United States. Rare indeed is the administration that escapes even the hint of impropriety.

The reasons why presidential scandals occur are many and varied. Some are the result of trying to hide secret operations, others are abuses of presidential power and privilege, and some occur because of emotions such as love or jealousy.

Often it is not the president himself who is involved in scandalous behavior, but rather aides or appointees who have betrayed the pub-

A Thomas Nast Cartoon of the "Whiskey Ring Corruption" scandal of 1876. Nast was a popular nineteenth-century political cartoonist.

lic trust and the privilege of their office. Perhaps these scandals are the inevitable result of people being given too much power and too much responsibility by the leader of the strongest nation in the world. Because no two people are the same, some perform admirably under such circumstances while others do not and become involved in scandal.

Thankfully, the scandals in most administrations have been minor in nature, and usually the events themselves have not directly involved the president. The United States is fortunate that most of its chief executives have behaved honorably while in office in keeping with the high expectations that the American people have for their president.

However, some administrations have been engulfed in scandal, and these are the ones that are the focus of this book. In the opinion of many, the five presidential administrations covered here in detail—those of Ulysses S. Grant, Warren G. Harding, Richard M. Nixon, Ronald Reagan, and Bill Clinton—are defined by the scandals that occurred during their terms as much as by each president's accomplishments. These administrations are the exception rather than the rule in American history, and we study them not only to learn from their mistakes but also to try and understand the reasons why these presidential terms are tainted by scandal.

CHAPTER 1

Presidential Scandals in Perspective

In 1887 English historian Lord Acton wrote a letter that contained one of the famous sayings of all time: "Power tends to corrupt, and absolute power corrupts absolutely. Great men are almost always bad men."[1]

Although he was not writing about the United States, Acton's observation can be applied to American democracy as easily as it can to any other style of government, in any other country of the world. Corruption in the highest levels of government, regardless of whether a nation is led by a king, czar, prime minister, dictator, or president, is a common thread throughout history. No government or country has been immune to scandal.

In ancient Greece the great philosopher Plato wrote that he had once wanted to enter politics but had changed his mind when he realized that such a life was full of corruption. During the height of the Roman Empire, ordinary citizens seemed resigned to the rampant corruption infecting their land. They suffered the likes of Caligula (reigned A.D. 37–41), who is reported to have spent 10 million sesterces (equal to about $1 million today) on a single banquet, and Nero (reigned A.D. 54–68), who tortured or executed people who displeased him and often wasted public monies on lavish banquets and parties.

Corruption and scandal have also plagued American politics at the highest levels, though not on a scale anywhere near that which existed in ancient Rome. Human weakness, greed, jealousy, and deceit have all surfaced at various times in American history, leading to scandalous acts by presidents and their advisers. Even some of the nation's most honored presidents had to deal with corruption and scandals that occurred during their time in office. Few presidential administrations have been immune to charges of scandal.

Scandals in Washington's Time

Even George Washington, revered for his role in America's founding, was accused of scandalous behavior while serving as the nation's first president. One sensational story, spread by political opponents, suggested that Secretary of the Treasury Alexander Hamilton was actually Washington's illegitimate son. Hamilton, the story went, was born of an affair in Barbados between Washington and a married woman.

Another charge leveled against President Washington was that he had stolen over four thousand dollars from the federal government by deliberately overdrawing his salary. Outraged by this and other attacks on his integrity, Washington wrote a bitter letter to Thomas Jefferson. In it he described his dismay at being referred to in "such exaggerated and indecent terms as could scarcely be applied to Nero, a notorious defaulter, or even a common pickpocket."[2]

Just as today, sex scandals also ensnared presidents and their advisers going back to Washington's time. In 1797 a sensational story emerged that former treasury secretary Alexander Hamilton, Washington's trusted adviser and a married man, several years earlier had had an affair with a married woman named Maria Reynolds, who blackmailed him to keep it quiet. To stop the story from being used against him, Hamilton published a ninety-seven-page pamphlet in which he admitted that it was true and expressed remorse. (Setting the bar for political wives for centuries to come, Elizabeth Hamilton gamely stuck by her husband after the affair became public, complimenting him on both his goodness and his genius.)

Sex scandals have continued to play a part in presidential politics ever since. In the 1800 election, President John Adams, happily married to his wife, Abigail, was accused of having sent General Thomas Pinckney to England to obtain four mistresses—two for Adams and two for Pinckney. When Adams heard this, he quipped, "I do declare if this be true, General Pinckney has kept them all for himself and cheated me out of my two."[3] Adams's successor, Thomas Jefferson, was accused of having affairs with several married women as well as with one of his slaves, Sally Hemings. (The debate over the relationship between Jefferson and Hemings still continues.)

The Petticoat War

In the 1828 presidential election, eventual winner Andrew Jackson was called an adulterer and a bigamist because his wife, Rachel, had not been legally divorced from her first husband when she married Jackson approximately forty years earlier. Although Rachel had believed the divorce was valid when she married Jackson, she was denounced as an adulteress during the campaign. The adverse publicity plunged her into a deep depression, and she died before

her husband's inauguration. On Inauguration Day, an embittered
Jackson wore a black armband
in her honor.

With the wounds of his
wife's death and her ruined
reputation still fresh, Jackson had to deal with an-
other scandal during his
administration, this one involving another married
woman: Peggy Eaton, the
wife of Secretary of War
John Eaton. Peggy was a vi-
vacious, fun-loving woman
with a flirtatious manner and
a fondness for low-cut dresses.
This, plus a past that included a
previous marriage and at least
one affair, dismayed many other
cabinet members and their wives as
well as the very proper
Washington social set.
Jackson's cabinet split into
pro– and anti–Peggy Eaton

*Opponents labeled Andrew Jackson an
adulterer and bigamist during the 1828
presidential campaign.*

factions, and the antagonism between the two threatened to disrupt government operations. The Petticoat War, as the rift came to be known,
only ended when Jackson demanded that the entire cabinet resign. After
this, the saying around Washington was, "To the next Cabinet—may
they all be bachelors . . . or leave their wives at home!"[4]

Changing Standards

Sex came to the forefront of another presidential campaign in 1884,
when it was revealed that Democratic candidate Grover Cleveland
had fathered an illegitimate child ten years earlier. Cleveland had
been one of several men dating the same woman, a department store
worker from Buffalo, New York. When she became pregnant, she
named Cleveland as the father because all of the other men she had
been dating were married. Cleveland, although not certain that the
child was his, graciously agreed to pay child support. During the
campaign, Republicans taunted Cleveland supporters with the cry of
"Ma! Ma! Where's my pa?" Cleveland, however, had the last laugh,
winning the election.

While sex has often been at the core of presidential scandals, sometimes details do not become public knowledge until well after a president's term has ended. For example, when President Franklin D. Roosevelt (FDR) died suddenly at Warm Springs, Georgia, on April 12, 1945, his female companion was not his wife, Eleanor, but his former lover and longtime friend, Lucy Mercer Rutherfurd. The details of FDR's relationship with Rutherfurd would have been the most sensational story to come out of his remarkably scandal-free administration had it emerged during his presidency.

However, at this time most journalists followed an unwritten code that decreed a president's private life to be off-limits. Thus, FDR's dalliance was not revealed to the public during his long four-term presidency. In a similar manner, the adulterous actions of both Presidents John F. Kennedy and Lyndon Johnson were also concealed from the public during their administrations. Only in more recent times have the details of these affairs become widely known.

When scandals arise involving presidents, presidential behavior is often to blame, and certainly this is the case in sexual affairs. However, sometimes the scandal that casts a shadow on the White House stems instead from the behavior of someone close to the president.

The Extravagant Ways of Mary Todd Lincoln

For Abraham Lincoln, scandal came from an unusual source: his wife, Mary Todd Lincoln. Her extravagant spending, particularly during the Civil War when many in the Union were sacrificing for the sake of the troops, caused her husband extreme embarrassment. She padded the White House expense account, claiming charges far in excess of the actual cost. For a state banquet for France's Emperor Napoleon III, she billed the Interior Department nine hundred dollars, although the actual cost was three hundred dollars. When the secretary of the interior rejected the charge, Mary forced her gardener to fake a bill for plants, flowers, and other implements for the amount, then certified the bill herself and kept the excess money. Her personal spending habits were so exorbitant that she was reportedly terrified that Lincoln would lose his 1864 re-election bid, leaving her with no income to pay off twenty-seven thousand dollars in bills she had accrued for personal purchases. "Mr. Lincoln has but little idea of the expense of a woman's wardrobe,"[5] she stated when asked to explain her outlandish personal spending.

But while Mary Lincoln may have been able to conceal her private purchases from her husband, her excessive use of public monies was not so easily hidden. After Congress appropriated twenty thousand dollars in 1861 to redecorate the White House,

Mary spent all of that—plus sixty-seven hundred dollars more. When she asked the president to get additional funds from Congress to cover the extra costs, Lincoln refused:

> I'll pay it out of my own pocket first. It would stink in the nostrils of the American people to have it said the President of the United States had approved a bill over-running an appropriation of $20,000 for flub dubs [pretentious items] for this damned old house, when the soldiers cannot have blankets.[6]

Congress did eventually provide the needed funds.

Mary Todd Lincoln's extravagant spending habits became a political issue during her husband's presidency.

Billy Carter's Libyan Connection

It was also a family member who caused a scandal for Democratic president Jimmy Carter. Billy Carter, the president's brother, was an affable man who enjoyed a good time.

In 1980, however, it was revealed that Billy had received $220,000 from the Libyan government as an initial payment on a $500,000 loan. Relations between the United States and Libya had been strained for several years. The United States had even recalled its ambassador to Libya, leaving the two nations with no formal means of communication. President Carter had also been applying pressure on Libya to cease its well-documented support of terrorist activities. Thus, the loan to Billy suggested that the North African nation was trying to influence the president by currying favor with a family member.

Billy Carter then compounded the problems for his brother. When asked why he was associating with a nation that supported terrorism, Billy said, "There's a helluva lot more Arabians than there is Jews,"[7] a thinly veiled reference to America's long-standing commitment to Israel. This remark outraged the American Jewish community.

"Billygate," as the media dubbed it, was a disaster for President Carter. Already crippled by an inflation-wracked economy and his inability to secure the release of fifty-three Americans taken hostage by Iranian militants, Carter's job approval rating sank to a rock bottom 22 percent. It did not help when Carter revealed that he had tried to use his brother as a backdoor ambassador to Libya, to see if that nation would use its influence to help free the American hostages. A subsequent Senate investigation failed to define the relationship between Billy Carter and Libya, but this backhanded vindication did not help the president, who lost his re-election bid to Ronald Reagan in November 1980.

Fearing for the Republic

Sometimes, however, presidents do not need relatives or associates to create scandal—they are quite capable of doing it all by themselves. This was the case with the fifteenth president, Democrat James Buchanan. In his 1857 inaugural address, Buchanan decried corruption, saying, "Next in importance to the maintenance of the Constitution and the Union is the duty of preserving the government free from the taint, or even the suspicion, of corruption."[8] Despite his impassioned description of presidential duties, Buchanan's administration was so scandal-ridden that one observer wondered if the country could survive under the weight of so much wrong doing.

Even before he was elected president, Buchanan promised to award lucrative naval contracts to his friend George Plitt, in exchange for campaign contributions. Once in office Buchanan continued to reward his supporters. In one instance, government contract deadlines were rigged so that only a Massachusetts man who had given over sixteen thousand dollars to the Buchanan campaign could meet them. In another, Buchanan received a letter urging him to give a fat government contract to a Philadelphia-based firm, which in turn promised to influence the 1858 re-election of Congressman Thomas Florence, one of the president's friends. Buchanan endorsed the letter, the contract was awarded, and Florence was reelected.

Even as the Union was splintering over slavery in the last desperate years before the Civil War, graft remained a high priority for the Buchanan administration. At this time all government documents were printed by the private sector. Buchanan made sure that his political friends received plenty of this lucrative business. Some of the money these firms made found its way back to the president in the form of campaign contributions.

The tawdry reputation of the Buchanan administration poisoned the nation's legitimate business dealings. A bill authorizing the United States to purchase Cuba from Spain for $30 million was withdrawn because of congressional concerns that some of the money would wind up in Buchanan's slush fund.

Finally, Congress grew tired of Buchanan's scandals and formally censured the president on June 13, 1860. Public revulsion over Buchanan's conduct not only sparked the nomination of "Honest Abe" Lincoln for president by the Republicans in 1860, but it also helped Lincoln win the election. As one observer said, "Our triumph was achieved more because of Lincoln's . . . honesty and the known corruption of the Democrats, than because of the negro question."[9]

Washington and Lincoln are presidents whom history holds in high regard today, yet both were touched by scandal. Another chief executive who belongs in that category is Thomas Jefferson.

The "Infidel" President

In addition to the sexual escapades charged against Jefferson, a serious controversy erupted over his religious beliefs—or lack thereof—during the 1800 presidential campaign.

Years before, Jefferson had been the driving force behind Virginia's Freedom of Religion Bill. It stipulated that "no man shall be compelled to frequent or support any religious worship."[10] From this simple statement, a precursor of the freedom of religion clause of the First Amendment, it was an easy step for political enemies to claim that Jefferson was an infidel and did not believe in God. The Jefferson religion scandal swept the country, threatening to destroy his presidential prospects. The Reverend John M. Mason identified "national regard or disregard of religion" as the main issue of the 1800 election. According to Mason, anyone voting for Jefferson "would do more to destroy the gospel of Jesus than a whole fraternity of infidels."[11]

Buchanan's administration was so scandal-ridden that Congress censured the president on June 13, 1860.

Although not a typical scandal inasmuch as it involved unpopular beliefs rather than wrongdoing, the controversy over Jefferson's religious views developed into a crisis. This happened because he would not respond to overwrought critics who accused him of being a godless monster. "From the clergy I expect no mercy," he wrote. "Ministers and merchants love nobody. . . . In every country and every age the priest has been hostile to liberty."[12]

Jefferson belonged to the Episcopal Church and often attended services. But his refusal to air his personal beliefs in public forums convinced many that he did indeed harbor dark designs against organized religion. This worried supporters of Jefferson's Democratic/Republican Party and very nearly cost the United States the services of one of its greatest leaders.

From minor flaps to constitutional crises, presidential scandals have been part of the political landscape ever since the birth of the American nation. The United States is fortunate that a large majority of its presidential administrations have been relatively free of gross wrongdoing. Some, however, were so awash in scandal that the misdeeds of a few presidents and their associates remain an indelible part of the historical record.

CHAPTER 2

Ulysses S. Grant

Ulysses S. Grant is considered one of the finest military commanders in American history. As a general in the Union army, and later as supreme commander of all Union forces, Grant demonstrated absolute self-confidence and determination. He acted decisively, fought aggressively, and never lost sight of the ultimate goal. For these and other qualities Grant is remembered as a great general.

Although initially not interested in politics, Grant rode his battlefield fame into the White House in 1868, succeeding Andrew Johnson. As president he signed bills ensuring voting rights for blacks and settled claims against Great Britain for damage done by British-built Confederate ships during the war, thus leading to a new era of cooperation between England and the United States.

Overall, however, the attributes that brought him military glory did not serve him well in the presidency. Grant was a soldier, not a politician. The self-confidence and decisiveness he demonstrated in the military did not transfer to civilian life. In the military his orders were obeyed without question; as a private citizen, con artists, wily politicians, and duplicitous friends with hidden agendas often ignored his desires. In business, he lacked the financial knowledge and common sense needed to succeed in even a simple investment. As a politician, he appointed numerous personal friends and acquaintances to important government positions—despite their lack of qualifications—and then stubbornly stuck by them, even to the point of not acknowledging their misdeeds after being presented with evidence of wrongdoing. Unfortunately, wrongdoing is what the Grant administration is most remembered for in the annals of history.

The Young Man from Ohio

Hiram Ulysses Grant was born on April 27, 1822, to Jesse and Hannah Grant of Point Pleasant, Ohio. The elder Grant ran a tannery, but young Ulysses (he preferred his middle name) had no desire to follow in his father's footsteps. He loved horses and could not abide the foul smell of the tannery, nor the screams of the animals as they were killed for their hides.

Grant also lacked his father's business sense. This problem surfaced early in his life and would recur many times in adulthood. On one occasion, young Ulysses wanted to buy a horse that a man was selling for $25. His father told him to first offer $20 for the horse, then $22.50, and, if neither of those bids was accepted, to agree to the full $25. But when Grant went to buy the horse, he repeated his father's entire set of instructions to the astonished seller. Naturally, the man held out for the $25.

When Jesse Grant realized that his son had no interest in working at the tannery, he arranged an appointment for him to West Point, the U.S. Military Academy. When seventeen-year-old Grant arrived at West Point in 1839, one of the first things he did was to rearrange his name, calling himself Ulysses H. Grant. However, due to a clerical error on the paperwork for his appointment, he was listed as Ulysses S. Grant. He never bothered to change it.

After graduating from West Point in 1843 (he ranked twenty-first out of a class of thirty-nine), Grant met Julia Dent, the sister of his roommate, Fred Dent. A romance blossomed but was interrupted when Grant served in the Mexican War (1845–1847). The couple married after the war, on August 22, 1848.

Dead-Ended in the Army

Unlike many other West Point graduates, who resigned to seek their fortune in the business world, Grant chose to remain in the army after marriage. Unfortunately for Grant, opportunities were few in a peacetime army; he was shuttled from one dead-end post to another with little hope of advancement. Moving from place to place was difficult on the newlyweds, who were trying to fashion a life together.

In the spring of 1852 Grant was transferred to the Columbia Barracks at Fort Vancouver, in what later became the Washington Territory. Julia could not make the trip with him because she was pregnant with their second child. (The first, a boy named Fred, was born in May 1850.) Instead, she went to have the baby at the home of Grant's parents in Bethel, Ohio.

Alone at the isolated post, Grant tried to focus on making money, as so many others were doing. It was just a few years after the California gold rush, and there was a sense of easy money in the air. "There is no reason why an active energetic person should not make a fortune every year,"[13] he confidently wrote Julia.

But Grant's optimism was premature. His numerous business ventures were plagued by bad luck and failure. When he tried to grow potatoes and oats, for example, a freak flood wiped out the crops and all hope of making a profit.

Worse yet, a habit of blindly trusting people led to disaster when Grant invested in a San Francisco store run by an acquaintance named Elijah Camp. Grant sank over fifteen hundred dollars in the business, and he foolishly destroyed the financial records of his investment because Camp claimed that he could not sleep nights worrying that Grant might want to collect his money before the store became successful. Inevitably, the business failed and Grant lost all of his money. A few years later, when Grant tried to find Camp to recover some of the lost funds, he found that the merchant had embarked on a sailing expedition—on a new boat. As Grant biographer William S. McFeely notes, "There was always an Elijah Camp in Ulysses Grant's business deals."[14]

Portrait of Ulysses S. Grant as a second lieutenant, taken shortly after his graduation from West Point.

Frustrated and depressed, Grant pined for his wife and children, particularly the newborn baby he had never seen. This was a time of stress in Grant's marriage, and letters from Julia were few and far between. Six months passed before Grant knew that the new baby was a boy, named Ulysses S. Grant Jr. Letters from home were so infrequent that Grant became angry. "Where mails come but twice per month it does seem as though I might expect news from you,"[15] he wrote his wife in June 1852.

In February 1854 Grant was transferred to Fort Humboldt in Northern California. The change of scenery did him little good. He missed his family, his business deals continued to fail, and he despised his senior officer. In despair, he started a letter to his wife with the line, "You do not know how forsaken I feel here."[16]

Finally, Grant gave up. He resigned from the army on July 31, 1854, and returned to his family. But the future looked bleak; at age thirty-two, Grant had left the only profession at which he had ever earned a living to once again try his hand at business.

Hardscrabble Years

In the spring of 1855 Grant received permission to work his brother-in-law's farm in eastern Missouri. He planted numerous crops, cleared land, and built a home he called "Hardscrabble." "Every day I like farming better and I do not doubt but that money is to be made at it,"[17] he wrote to his father.

But again he had more enthusiasm than success. He and his family barely survived on the meager income the farm generated. In desperation Grant cut firewood and hauled it into St. Louis. There, he sold it on street corners, standing shivering and sullen in the wind and cold, wrapped in his fading blue army overcoat. Urgent appeals to his father for loans to help him buy tools and other farming necessities went unanswered. At the end of 1857 Grant's financial situation was so dire that he was forced to pawn his gold watch for twenty-two dollars.

By 1858, with the farm generating virtually no income, Grant had to face reality. "Without means, it is useless for me to go on farming,"[18] he said. He sold the farm in exchange for a house in St. Louis, where he went into business with one of Julia's cousins as a bill collector. Grant hated the work, but he could not find another job. With no prospects, his only option was to once again seek his father's help.

A Helping Hand

Grant returned to his family's home during the winter of 1859–1860. At age thirty-seven it devastated him to admit that he still needed his father's assistance, and he was plagued by severe headaches upon his return. When he first arrived home he sat silently in the dining room, paralyzed by depression and anxiety. Fortunately, this time his father did provide a helping hand, offering Grant a job selling leather goods in the family store in Galena, Illinois. In the summer of 1860 Grant moved his family to Galena and began yet another new career.

Ulysses S. Grant might have spent the rest of his life as a sales clerk were it not for the Civil War. The war began in April 1861 with an attack by Confederate forces on Union-occupied Fort Sumter in Charleston, South Carolina. Patriotic fervor exploded throughout both the North and the South as men rushed to enlist in the armed forces. In Galena, during a troop recruitment meeting, someone noted that Grant was a West Point graduate and the only one present with military experience. He was elected to chair the meeting, and it was the turning point of his life. From that moment on, his past failures were swept away. He turned his back on his clerk's job and never looked back. As Grant later recalled, "I never went into our leather store after that meeting, to put up a package or do other business."[19]

Unconditional Surrender Grant

Grant rejoined the Union army as a colonel. By August, thanks to the federal government's desperate need for seasoned officers to lead the inexperienced volunteer troops, he was promoted to brigadier general.

Grant now began one of the most remarkable rises to prominence in American military history. While his counterparts in the

Grant's pre–Civil War home in Galena, Illinois.

Eastern theater of war suffered defeat after defeat at the hands of poorly equipped Confederate troops commanded by Robert E. Lee, Grant made a name for himself in the West by repeatedly winning battles. He began this string of successes in February 1862 by defeating the rebels at both Fort Henry and Fort Donelson on the Tennessee River. These were the first major Union victories of the war.

At Fort Donelson, Grant acquired a nickname that remained with him throughout the war and further increased his fame. The Confederate commander was Simon Buckner, Grant's old friend from West Point who had once loaned Grant money to help him through some rough times. When Buckner realized that his situation was hopeless, he asked Grant for surrender terms, hoping that their friendship would result in leniency for himself and his men. However, Grant quickly proved that wartime voided old intimacies, replying tersely, "No terms except an unconditional and immediate surrender can be accepted. I propose to move immediately upon your works."[20] Because his initials were *U. S.*, Grant became known as "Unconditional Surrender" Grant. This hard-line attitude boosted the spirits of the hero-starved Union and marked Grant as a rising star in the Union army.

General Grant arriving at Confederate headquarters to accept the surrender of Vicksburg during the Civil War.

Grant's growing reputation even withstood periodic disasters. In April 1862, at the Battle of Shiloh (also known as Pittsburg Landing) in western Tennessee, Grant's forces were surprised by the Confederates and nearly routed. After receiving reinforcements overnight, Grant counterattacked the next day and drove the rebels from the battlefield. The tremendous number of casualties at Shiloh stunned the nation (approximately twenty-three-thousand men from both sides were killed or wounded, more than the combined total of American casualties from the Revolutionary War, the War of 1812, and the Mexican War). Although Grant ultimately won the battle, the casualty rate and the near-destruction of his army at Shiloh unleashed a torrent of criticism. But to those who demanded that he be replaced, President Abraham Lincoln had a succinct answer: "I can't spare this man. He fights."[21]

Lieutenant General

On July 4, 1863, Grant won his greatest military victory. After a siege of over five weeks, the previously impregnable Confederate town of Vicksburg, Mississippi, surrendered to Grant. This gave the Union control of the Mississippi River and split the Confederacy in half. Grant accomplished the fall of Vicksburg by marching his army south on the opposite side of the Mississippi River, then crossing the water via Union gunboats and defeating Southern troops in several battles, forcing them to flee to Vicksburg. After trying and failing to storm the city, Grant laid siege to the city and waited for hunger and desperation to bring him victory—which it did.

Grant continued his spectacular rise. After achieving victory at Chattanooga, Tennessee, in the autumn of 1863, Grant was made a lieutenant general—the same rank as George Washington. In March 1864 he was given command of all Union forces.

With all units under his control, Grant embarked on a strategy to expose the South's greatest weaknesses. Confederate forces were poorly equipped and less numerous than Union forces, so in the spring of 1864 Grant initiated simultaneous offensive campaigns aimed at depleting the already strained Confederate resources. Grant himself took on the challenge of fighting the wily Confederate general Robert E. Lee, sending the Union's Army of the Potomac into a series of pitched battles with Lee and his army in the East. Despite deficiencies in men and material Lee inflicted terrible losses on Grant, such as at the Battle of the Wilderness in Virginia, where the Union lost more than seventeen thousand men and gained no territory.

Instead of retreating northward as others had done after suffering defeats by Lee, Grant pushed south toward the Confederate capital of Richmond. Lee had no alternative but to use his dwindling forces to protect Richmond. From May 8 to 19, 1864, the two sides fought every day. Each battle drained strength from the Confederate army.

Again, the large numbers of casualties that this strategy induced brought protests against Grant's leadership. At Cold Harbor in Virginia, seven thousand Union soldiers fell in thirty minutes in an ill-advised assault on Lee's well-entrenched troops. Northern families felt their sons were being sacrificed and blamed "the Butcher Grant," as he was called. Writing about the terrible loss of life, poet Walt Whitman said at the time, "I steadily believe that Grant is going to succeed, and that we shall have Richmond—but oh what a price to pay for it."[22]

As another way of exhausting Southern manpower, Grant ended the prisoner-exchange system, whereby captured soldiers on both sides were released in equal numbers and returned to their units. As Grant explained,

> Every man we hold, when released on parole or otherwise, becomes an active soldier against us at once either directly or indirectly. If we commence a system of exchanges which liberates all prisoners taken, we will have to fight on until the whole South is exterminated.[23]

The halting of prisoner exchanges exacted a huge toll on Union as well as Confederate soldiers. The South, with barely enough food for its own citizens, simply did not have the resources to feed and care for growing numbers of Union prisoners. The death rate skyrocketed among captive Union soldiers, and many Northerners protested against what they considered Grant's callous disregard for his men.

Eventually, however, Grant's strategy paid off. Faced with vastly superior numbers, Lee surrendered to Grant at Appomattox Courthouse on April 9, 1865. After four bloody years, the Civil War was finally over.

A New Career

Grant's popularity soared in the North, but there was little for a fighter to do in a peacetime army. Inevitably, talk arose of him running for president. Although he was not a politician, the presidency may have seemed an attractive option to Grant. Only in his midforties and with no other job prospects, the presidency would at least offer financial stability for his family.

In May 1868 the Republicans nominated Grant for president. In the general election in November he defeated Democratic candidate

A May 1868 Republican Party poster touted Grant for president and Schuyler Colfax for vice president.

Horatio Seymour, though by only a slim margin. Grant tallied 3 million votes to Seymour's 2.7 million.

Grant's Inexperience Shows

When he accepted the Republican presidential nomination, Grant had said, "Let us have peace."[24] To a nation weary of both the Civil War and the increasingly venomous political bickering that marked Reconstruction, Grant's election offered hope that peace was indeed at hand. America, in fact, did not engage in another war during Grant's administration. Unfortunately, his presidency was anything but peaceful.

One of his first acts as president, appointing a cabinet, was a process marked by missteps and misplaced loyalties. It set the tone for the rest of his presidency. Instead of choosing qualified people for his cabinet, Grant appointed old friends—some of whom had no qualifications for the positions they were given.

Grant's first choice for secretary of state, Congressman Elihu Washburne, was completely unfamiliar with law and diplomacy. His only qualification for the post was that he was a longtime Grant supporter. Eleven days later Hamilton Fish, a respected, intelligent man who had formerly served as a U.S. senator and the governor of New York, replaced Washburne. For secretary of the treasury Grant initially wanted his friend Alexander T. Stewart, a rich New York businessman. When told that the law forbade the treasury secretary to be engaged in business, Grant asked the Senate to ignore it. When that request was refused, Grant replaced Stewart with George Boutwell, a Massachusetts congressman with no interest or expertise in financial matters. Initially Grant asked John M. Schofield, secretary of war under President Andrew Johnson, to remain at his post. A few days later, however, John A. Rawlins, a Civil War confidant of Grant's, replaced Schofield.

Black Friday

Grant's flawed choices for cabinet posts demonstrated two aspects of his personality: He believed loyalty deserved to be rewarded, and he placed absolute trust in the advice and counsel of loyal friends. Unfortunately, many of those whom he entrusted with running the country or turned to for advice, did not merit that trust. This became apparent early in his presidency, in the sequence of events that culminated in Black Friday.

In the spring of 1869, financier Jay Gould tried to corner the New York City gold supply in order to drive up the price and make an enormous profit. However, Gould knew that the federal government could shatter his scheme by selling some of its vast gold holdings, thus increasing the supply and lowering prices. For his plan to work, Gould had to know whether Grant's administration would step in and sell gold or would let the price rise according to market forces.

Gould enlisted Grant's brother-in-law, Abel R. Corbin, to help him convince the president that having the government sell gold was bad for the country. Several times over the next few months Corbin and

Gould met with Grant and warned him of the dire consequences of selling government gold: a shrinking economy, reduced sales for farmers, financial hardship, and even armed revolution. If Grant knew that he was being manipulated, he never let on.

Convinced that he and Corbin had swayed the president, in the late summer of 1869 Gould (later aided by financier Jim Fisk), began buying large amounts of gold. As the gold supply shrank, the price rose; financiers and speculators knew that the market was being manipulated and also bought gold, gambling that they would be able to sell it at an even higher price. Stocks, which usually moved in direct opposition to the price of gold, plummeted. Financial markets around the world were thrown into a tizzy, wondering how high the U.S. price of gold was going to rise.

Finally, Grant realized he had been duped by both Corbin and Gould. Worse yet, he found out that Corbin's wife—his sister—was involved in gold speculation. On Friday, September 24, the federal government dumped $4 million worth of gold onto the market. Instantly the price plummeted, and many who had bought gold at great expense were ruined when the price fell. The day became known as Black Friday. Corbin was disgraced, and the assistant secretary of the treasury, Daniel Butterfield, who was also part of the scheme, resigned. Although Grant had no part in the scheme, Black Friday illustrates his misplaced trust in those close to him. It also demonstrates his political naïveté; a more astute politician might have suspected that Corbin and Gould had a hidden agenda. Though keen insight had helped Grant defeat Robert E. Lee, one of history's cleverest generals, that quality seems to have been absent from Grant's presidency.

Jay Gould, a businessman whose speculation brought about the collapse of the gold market.

Santo Domingo

Besides a lack of political savvy, Grant also brought to the presidency unrealistic expectations. As a general, he was accustomed to having his orders obeyed without question. As president, he discovered that the civilian world operated very differently. For instance, early in his administration Grant decided that he wanted to annex the Dominican Republic, or Santo Domingo, as he called it. He felt that by adding this country to the United States, a naval base could be built there to protect American interests in the Caribbean. Despite intense lobbying by Grant, a treaty to annex Santo Domingo was rejected by the Senate. Many senators disapproved because annexation would have eliminated self-government in Santo Domingo, which at the time was one of just two black-led republics in the world.

A political cartoon from 1874 pokes fun at The Whiskey Ring, a group of government agents who took bribes from alcohol distillers and distributors.

IN FOR IT.
U. S. "I hope I shall get to the bottom soon."

Scandal also played a part in the treaty's failure. It was revealed that Grant's close friend and personal secretary, Orville Babcock, who had vigorously lobbied the president to annex the island, had been secretly given land on Santo Domingo that would have become more valuable if the country became part of the United States. Despite evidence of impropriety on Babcock's part, Grant stubbornly refused to believe that his friend was guilty of any wrongdoing.

Second-Term Woes

Although corruption had plagued his first administration, Grant was overwhelmingly elected to a second presidential term in 1872, primarily due to a strong economy. He was also aided by disarray among the Democrats, who did not field a candidate of their own but instead supported the reform ticket of liberal Republican candidate Horace Greeley.

Even before Grant's second term began, however, another controversy erupted that demonstrated his lack of understanding of politics and the public's view of politicians. On the last day of his first term, Grant signed a bill doubling his own pay from twenty-five to fifty thousand dollars and boosting the salaries of Congress and the Supreme Court justices. In addition, the bill included a five thousand dollar "bonus" for each member of Congress, including those defeated in the previous election, representing a retroactive salary increase for the two years previously served. Grant signed this legislation, derisively dubbed the Salary Grab Act, without comment, but public outrage forced Congress to repeal all salary increases except those for the president and Supreme Court justices.

The Salary Grab Act was a harbinger of Grant's scandal-filled second term. In June 1874 Treasury Secretary William Richardson resigned after it was revealed that he had allowed a tax collector to keep 50 percent of the delinquent taxes he had received from citizens, defrauding the government of $213,500. When the House Ways and Means Committee declared that Richardson deserved severe condemnation and recommended that Grant remove him, the president complied but made him a U.S. Court of Claims judge.

The Whiskey Ring

A far more serious scandal was the so-called Whiskey Ring. In the autumn of 1874, Treasury Secretary Benjamin Bristow (who had replaced Richardson) discovered that government tax agents were taking bribes from alcohol distillers and distributors. Among those involved were General John McDonald, an old friend of Grant's who had been appointed collector of internal revenue for the St. Louis region, and Orville Babcock. Grant again ignored evidence that his

William H. Belknap, Grant's secretary of war, who was forced to resign in the wake of scandal.

friends were corrupt, even telling an incredulous Bristow that McDonald "was one honest man upon whom they [Grant and Bristow] could rely."[25] Grant had no idea that McDonald, at that very moment, was in New York, ready to flee the country by ship because he feared arrest.

McDonald eventually went to prison for his role in the Whiskey Ring scandal. However, Babcock was acquitted at his trial, largely thanks to a deposition by Grant proclaiming his secretary's innocence. Although Grant tried to have Babcock return to work as if nothing had happened, pressure from other cabinet members forced him to resign. Blinded by friendship, the president never forgave Bristow for exposing the Whiskey Ring and causing him to lose Babcock.

Throughout his presidency, Grant had shown himself either unwilling or unable to accept evidence of impropriety in friends who were serving in government posts. This occurred again with the most sensational scandal of Grant's second term, which involved Secretary of War William Belknap. Congressional investigators found that Belknap had received over twenty thousand dollars from selling the right to disburse supplies to the Indians. The money had primarily gone to his first and second wives for entertaining their Washington, D.C., friends.

Belknap resigned when the scandal became public. He was also impeached by the House of Representatives, but he was acquitted in the Senate. He lived the rest of his life in disgrace. As had happened so often in the past, Grant blamed his friend's downfall on political enemies trying to embarrass him. To Grant, it was truly astonishing that people could moralize about and condemn the actions of those they did not know, all evidence of unethical behavior to the contrary.

"Errors in Judgement"

As the end of his second term drew near, Grant was upset that Republican officials had no desire to nominate him for a third term. It was not one particular scandal but rather the cumulative effects of all of the scandals, however, that caused Republican Party leaders and the country in general to seek a fresh face for the White House.

Possibly sensing that he had let down both his party and his country, during his final State of the Union address on December 5, 1876, Grant tried to explain how things had gone so wrong. In the speech he blamed what he called "errors in judgement" on his lack of political training. Yet he was quick to seek refuge in historical precedent: "History shows that no Administration from the time of Washington to the present has been free from these mistakes."[26]

Final Years

As his second presidential term came to a close, Grant felt lost. Public service, in the military and as president, was all he knew. The thought of having to once again compete in private enterprise was daunting. Instead of trying, Grant and his wife went on a two-and-a-half-year trip around the world. He hoped that this journey would cleanse his reputation and make him the front-runner for the 1880 Republican presidential nomination. However, the memory of his scandal-ridden administration was too fresh, and he lost to Congressman James A. Garfield, who went on to be elected president.

In 1883 Grant gave the business world another try. He invested one hundred thousand dollars in a Wall Street brokerage firm run by his son Ulysses Jr. and Ferdinand Ward, a financial speculator who was considered one of the rising superstars of Wall Street. But Grant's luck was running true to form: Ward had used dishonest tactics to obtain bank loans. Ultimately the firm collapsed. The former president, along with many other investors, suffered financial ruin. As one observer later noted, Grant seemed "to be a perfect child in financial matters."[27]

Now without means for providing for himself and his family, Grant suffered a final blow when he was diagnosed with throat cancer in mid-1884. The last year of his life was a desperate race against death, as Grant sought to provide financial security for his family by writing his memoirs before the disease claimed him. Toward the end of his life, wracked with pain but consumed with the need to complete his book, he wrote,

Grant on the porch of his house in Mt. McGregor. This photo was taken three days before his death on July 23, 1885.

I do not sleep though I sometimes doze a little. If up I am talked to and in my efforts to answer cause pain. The fact is I think I am a verb instead of a personal pronoun. A verb is anything that signifies to be; to do; or to suffer. I signify all three.[28]

Surviving on sheer will alone, the old soldier won his last battle, finishing his book on July 14, 1885. He died one week later. His book earned several hundred thousand dollars in royalties, providing Julia Grant with financial security until her death in 1902.

Ulysses S. Grant was not a dishonest man, but he was unable to see dishonesty in others, especially those whom he trusted. Sadly, the scandalous actions of people willing to exploit the office of the president for their own gain have forever marred the reputation of one of the great generals in American history.

CHAPTER 3

Warren G. Harding

Warren G. Harding began his administration by saying, "I cannot hope to be one of the great presidents, but perhaps I may be remembered as one of the best loved."[29] Today, Harding is indeed remembered, but not with affection. His two and a half years are considered one of the worst presidencies in U.S. history.

Although honest, well-intentioned, friendly, and gracious, Harding seemed unable to grasp the complicated issues facing the president. Compounding his difficulties, Harding was betrayed by those whom he considered friends and appointed to office.

Perhaps because of the many problems he faced as president, Harding's administration had few accomplishments. The most notable was an international disarmament meeting held in Washington, D.C., in 1921 and 1922 that produced several treaties fostering greater international cooperation.

During his final months in office, Harding sought to reverse the damage done to his administration by scandal. He urged abolishment of the twelve-hour workday and seven-day workweek, called for the end of child labor, and advocated an investigation into the high cost of living.

No amount of last minute campaigning could save Harding's reputation, however. His term in office is notable for his lack of insight despite his years in politics. Harding's initial reluctance to run for president and his oft-stated fears that he was not up to the job reveal one of the few insights he had about his role as president. As his statements illustrate, Harding had no illusions about becoming a great president. Ultimately, he was proven right.

One of the Boys

Warren Gamaliel Harding was born on November 1, 1865, in Blooming Grove, Ohio. His parents were George Tryon Harding and Phoebe Harding. George Harding was a restless man, always ready to jump at what he imagined was a better opportunity. During his professional life he was a teacher, veterinarian, and finally a country doctor, more likely to be paid in chickens and butter than in cash. As a result of George's restlessness, the Hardings were almost always short of money. Phoebe supplemented the family's meager income by working as a nurse and midwife.

As a boy Warren was placid and serene, wanting only to fit in with his childhood group of friends. This desire to be one of the boys would mark his life, as would an inability to say no. Harding went to great lengths to avoid hurting a person's feelings, and so he tended to go along rather than take action that might lead to disappointment. Later, when his administration was in tatters, this tendency led to a saying that the difference between Harding and George Washington was that Washington could not tell a lie, and Harding could not tell a liar.

Marion and the *Star*

Although he had some of his father's restlessness, Harding channeled his energy into one outlet: the newspaper business. In 1884, after his family moved to Marion, Ohio, the teenage Harding and two partners bought a tiny struggling newspaper called the *Star*. Gregarious and friendly, Harding became a popular figure in town. This popularity, plus Harding's editorial skill, helped the newspaper thrive.

Harding's success with the *Star* put him squarely in the public eye of the growing town. A handsome man in his early twenties and the owner of a prosperous business, Harding was one of Marion's most eligible bachelors. Florence Kling DeWolfe, the divorced daughter of Amos Kling, Marion's wealthiest citizen, took notice of Harding. DeWolfe was a stern, sharp-tongued, superstitious woman whom Harding called "Duchess." She used her forceful personality to fervently woo Harding, and her determination ultimately triumphed over his initial nonchalance toward her. On July 8, 1891, the two were married in her spacious home in Marion. In keeping with her superstitious nature, Florence insisted that the eight o'clock

Warren G. Harding, the twenty-ninth president of the United States

The offices of the Marion Star, *a newspaper owned by Harding and the place where he got his start writing about Ohio politics.*

ceremony end before eight-thirty since she believed it was unlucky to do anything important during the second half of an hour.

Behind the prickly personality and superstitions (she believed that it was good luck if a cricket sang in your home, and she had servants catch them and place them in a special wooden box inside her house), Florence was a good businesswoman. She handled the business operations of the *Star*, reorganizing the paper's carrier-delivery system and implementing bookkeeping improvements.

Politics Beckon

The *Star*'s reputation grew both locally and statewide. It became an influential voice in Ohio's Republican politics. After a while Ohio Republicans began courting Harding as a possible candidate for public office, primarily because of his noncombative nature. At the time, the party was dominated by several strong personalities; frequent infighting and shifting alliances among the party bosses caused loyal Republican Theodore Roosevelt to remark, "I think there is only one thing in the world I cannot understand, and that is Ohio politics."[30]

In Harding, the Republicans saw a man who shunned controversy and got along with everyone. As he told *Star* employees, "There are two sides to every question. Get them both."[31] With his gift for oratory and ability to easily make friends, Harding seemed a natural for public office. In 1898 he climbed the first step on the political ladder by being elected as a state senator from Ohio's thirteenth district.

After winning another term in the Ohio Senate, Harding was elected lieutenant governor in 1903. Now a leading figure in Ohio politics, Harding continued to shun controversy and always searched for a middle ground. He tried to be, as biographer Francis Russell says, "most things to most men."[32] In the often-quarrelsome world of Ohio Republican politics, this made Harding stand out, and others took notice of him. At one point, in writing about a Republican state convention, the Cleveland *Plain Dealer* noted, "[Harding] made the delegate believe the word *harmony* had been written with indelible ink."[33]

Despite his growing reputation and popularity, Harding was not renominated for lieutenant governor in 1905 because party leaders wanted someone from southern Ohio to balance the ticket and fend off a fierce Democratic challenge for the state house. (The Republicans lost anyway in November.) Harding returned to Marion.

Five years later, in 1910, Harding received the Republican nomination for governor of Ohio. Befitting his reputation, Harding was a compromise candidate, chosen only when the party could not agree on any of several others. Despite running a vigorous campaign, Harding was trounced in November by his Democratic rival. However, in an upbeat letter to a friend a few days after the election, he seemed almost relieved that he did not win. He wrote that he had had the germ of running for political office eradicated from his system and was now free to do other things that pleased him more than searching for men of "abiding honesty"[34] to appoint to office.

The letter is revealing, for it shows Harding's lack of ambition for political office and his contentment with spending time at more amiable pursuits. But he was soon to be plunged into the political world once again.

"This Is the Zenith of My Political Ambition"

In June 1912 incumbent president and fellow Ohioan William Howard Taft asked Harding to nominate him for a second presidential term at the Republican convention in Chicago. During the campaign Harding showed his party loyalty by vigorously campaigning for Taft against Democrat Woodrow Wilson and former president Theodore Roosevelt, who had bolted the Republicans and was running as a third-party candidate.

Although Taft lost, Harding emerged as one of the top Republicans in Ohio. In 1914 he was selected to run for the U.S. Senate. He won the election by over one hundred thousand votes and happily told the crowd gathered in front of his Marion home, "This is the zenith of my political ambition."[35]

Harding's Senate career was undistinguished. During his five years in office he introduced 134 bills; 122 of these concerned local affairs in Ohio, such as securing a veteran's pension or renaming a ship. The remaining 12 bills with a national focus were trivial, such as celebrating the Pilgrims' landing.

As a senator, Harding followed the pattern he had established early in his career: trying to appease everyone and offend no one. Rarely did he take a stand on any important issue of the day. In

Harding as a U.S. senator in 1919. The death of Theodore Roosevelt that same year changed Harding's life.

1916, when a group of women demanded to know whether he supported female suffrage (a woman's right to vote), Harding replied that he would prefer that the Republican Party state a position for him to follow rather than him having to "assume a leadership or take an individual position on the question."[36]

Although he had little impact in legislative matters, Harding enjoyed the Senate, particularly its camaraderie—drinking, poker playing, and storytelling with other politicians. Uninspired by the hard work of proposing and passing new legislation, Harding found other uses for his time in Washington.

When, in 1905, a kidney ailment forced his wife to remain in bed, Harding began an affair with Carrie Phillips, the wife of a close friend. The affair continued for several years, until Phillips moved to Berlin, Germany, in search of a more cosmopolitan atmosphere than Marion, Ohio, could offer.

Around this time Harding met Nan Britton. Britton had developed a crush on Harding at age thirteen while still a schoolgirl in Marion. In her school notebook, Britton had written love-struck verse such as "Warren Gamaliel Harding—he's a darling."[37] By the end of July 1917, Britton (now twenty) and Harding became lovers. While at his desk in the Senate, as critical issues concerning World War I were debated, Harding composed long, rambling love letters to Britton. Sometimes he brought her to his office in the Senate building for passionate interludes. In January 1919 Britton became pregnant. On October 22, 1919, she gave birth to a daughter, whom she named Elizabeth Ann. Harding never acknowledged that the child was his (although Britton identified him as the father in a book published after Harding's death).

Harding's life might have continued this way if not for the death of Theodore Roosevelt on January 6, 1919. At the time of his death (from natural causes), the former president was the overwhelming favorite for the 1920 Republican presidential nomination. His death threw the party into disarray and opened the field for numerous other candidates. No Republican had ever won the presidency without winning Ohio, so it was natural that party leaders looked to Harding as the potential nominee.

Harding, however, had no desire to be president. He wrote to a friend that he was happy to stay a senator, play golf, and enjoy himself. The burdens of the presidency were not for him. He was also concerned that a high-profile campaign might expose his extramarital affairs. He knew that word of these affairs could sink any hope of attaining the presidency.

The Smoke-Filled Room

But Harry Daugherty, an influential lawyer, political power broker, and lobbyist from Ohio, was unconcerned by such obstacles. Daugherty had first met Harding when the latter was campaigning for the Ohio Senate. According to one account, after meeting Harding for the first time, Daugherty had said, "Gee, what a great-looking president he'd make."[38]

Now, with the Republican Party in confusion, Daugherty decided to turn his vision into reality. He began a relentless campaign to convince Harding that he could win the nomination. Finally, Daugherty's efforts paid off. In early December 1919, Harding announced his candidacy for the Republican presidential nomination.

At the time, Harding's entry into the race only served to further crowd the field of possible nominees, which were led by front-runners General Leonard Wood and Illinois governor Frank O. Lowden. Harding seemed like the longest of long shots.

But Daugherty, with keen political foresight, thought that the two favorites might cancel each other out, thus opening the field for Harding. With eerie prescience, he told two reporters well before the convention,

> I don't expect Senator Harding to be nominated on the first, second, or third ballot, but I think about eleven minutes after two o'clock on Friday morning of the convention, when fifteen or twenty men, bleary-eyed and perspiring profusely from the heat, are sitting around a table some one will say: "Who will we nominate?" At that decisive time the friends of Senator Harding can suggest him and can afford to abide by the result.[39]

This is precisely what happened. After four ballots, neither Wood nor Lowden could get a majority at the 1920 Republican convention, and it seemed that the stalemate would go on indefinitely. In frustration, Republican Party leaders met on the evening of June 11 in a suite at Chicago's Blackstone Hotel, a place that would become known in American political history as "the smoke-filled room." No matter how many times the party leaders evaluated the possible candidates, the one who always surfaced was Harding. He was from a key state, he had few enemies, he was a good public speaker, and he was handsome and distinguished-looking. Best of all, he was a simple man, the opposite of the scholarly current president, Democrat Woodrow Wilson, whose high-handed style had turned off many voters.

*Portrait of Nan Britton and her daughter Elizabeth Ann. Britton published
a book that claimed her daughter was fathered by Harding.*

Sometime around 2 A.M., Harding was summoned to the hotel
suite and told he was going to be nominated. Journalist George
Harvey said to Harding,

> We think you should tell us, on your conscience and before
> God, whether there is anything that might be brought up
> against you that would embarrass the party, any impedi-
> ment that might disqualify you or make you inexpedient,
> either as a candidate or as President.[40]

Harding asked for ten minutes to think this over and excused
himself from the room. What he did, alone, during those ten minutes has been the source of intense speculation. Some have suggested that he called both Nan Britton and Carrie Phillips and
satisfied himself that neither would reveal details of her affair with

him if he ran. After his ten minutes were up, Harding told the party leaders that he had nothing to hide.

Thus, Harding became the Republican presidential candidate in 1920. When asked to describe his surprising success at the convention, the card-loving Harding used a poker metaphor: "We drew to a pair of deuces and filled."[41]

A Return to Normalcy

During the presidential campaign against Democrat James Cox, Republican leaders realized that Harding had not been honest with them about having nothing to hide. When they learned of his affair with Phillips, they gave her twenty thousand dollars, plus a two thousand dollar monthly fee, and sent her and her husband on a cruise around the world that lasted until after Harding's inauguration.

With that threat removed, Harding was free to conduct his campaign, which he did from his front porch in Marion, promising America a return to normalcy. Weary from the upheaval wrought by the recently completed world war, the fight over the League of Nations, and domestic battles over issues such as women's suffrage and Prohibition, the nation responded eagerly to Harding's folksy promise to calm things down. He won a resounding victory over Cox, with 61 percent of the popular vote.

Overwhelmed

Initially Harding enjoyed his tenure as the nation's chief executive. "Being President," he commented early in his administration, "is an easy job."[42] But soon the demands of the office overwhelmed him. He lacked knowledge about the important issues of the day and had little desire to study and learn about them. As his confidence faded, his anxiety increased. "I am not fit for this office and should never have been here,"[43] he said to a friend.

Under the watchful eyes of servants, secretaries, and Secret Service agents, Harding had little privacy. "I'm in jail," he told Britton during one of her infrequent visits to the White House, "and I can't get out."[44] He longed to return to the easy story-swapping, card-playing life of his Senate days. One evening, when some high-ranking government officials were in a hotel suite getting ready to play poker, the door opened to reveal Harding. "You fellows can't sneak off and have a party without me,"[45] he said petulantly.

Harding made his own job harder by making some disastrous political appointments. For secretary of the interior he chose Albert Fall, a well-known anticonservationist and old friend from the Senate. Political deal maker Harry Daugherty was named attorney general, primarily because Harding could not refuse when his friend asked for the post. Both of these appointments would come back to haunt him, as would others. Harding gave jobs to many friends and acquaintances— often based on someone else's recommendation, and usually without checking their background.

Betrayed

It did not take long for Harding's carelessness to catch up to him. In the spring of 1922 Minnesota congressman Oscar Keller called for Daugherty's impeachment, filing a long list of charges against the attorney general with the House Committee on the Judiciary. Soon after this, the Senate Committee on Public Lands

Charles Forbes, director of the Veterans Bureau, pocketed up to $250 million of government money.

began an investigation into irregularities involving Fall's management of government oil reserves.

Harding tried to dismiss these allegations as politically motivated. But even the president had to face the truth when a scandal broke concerning Charles Forbes, director of the Veterans Bureau.

Another of Harding's poker-playing buddies, Forbes was selling government supplies from a medical supply base to a private contractor at incredibly low prices (rolls of gauze that cost $1.33 each for 26¢, new sheets costing $1.27 for 27¢, etc.) and getting a kickback on the profits. At the same time, many government hospitals were struggling with a shortage of supplies for their patients. Forbes also inflated the cost of building government hospitals and took a large percentage of the excess monies. Some sources claim that Forbes illegally pocketed $250 million from his schemes.

In late January 1923, when Harding discovered Forbes's swindles, he summoned him to the White House. There, he grabbed Forbes by the throat and cursed him for double-crossing him. Forbes fled to Europe and resigned from office. On March 2 the Senate began an investigation into irregularities at the Veterans Bureau. On March 16, 1923, Charles F. Cramer, general counsel of the Veterans Bureau and a partner in Forbes's illegal activities, committed suicide before he was scheduled to testify at a congressional hearing.

The Forbes scandal affected Harding deeply. His wife said that he "never recovered from Forbes's betrayal of himself and the administration."[46] Harding commented that he could take care of his enemies, but that his friends kept him walking the floor at night. As his worries mounted, his health suffered: his blood pressure rose, he lacked stamina and energy, and his drinking increased.

The Ohio Gang

As shocking as the Forbes affair was, it was soon overshadowed by another scandal. In late May 1923, Jess Smith, a friend and personal aide to Attorney General Daugherty, was found dead in his room, an apparent suicide. Smith had been routinely receiving bribes from the awarding of liquor licenses, selling paroles, and "fixing" things for people in trouble with the Justice Department. Once he showed his girlfriend a money belt stuffed with thousand-dollar bills. Rumors swirled around Washington that Smith had not killed himself but had been murdered because he knew too much about Daugherty's illegal activities.

Smith had been a pivotal member of the so-called Ohio Gang— a group of friends brought to Washington by Daugherty from his home state. Operating out of Smith's house, the group provided service and protection to bootleggers, sold withdrawal permits (which enabled alcohol to be removed from storage for medicinal purposes without running afoul of Prohibition), and practiced other larcenous ventures.

Depressed and heartsick by the growing scandals, Harding tried to buckle down to his duties. But as before, the complexities of the job proved beyond him. Once, while trying to understand a complicated tax bill, he cried in desperation to a friend, "Somewhere there must be a book that tells all about it, where I could go to straighten it out in my mind. But I don't know where the book is, and maybe I couldn't read it if I found it!"[47]

Last Journey

In late June 1923, Harding embarked on an arduous fifteen-hundred-mile journey across the United States. His purpose was twofold: to rally public opinion behind his desire for the United States to join the World Court, a judicial body composed of various countries that would arbitrate international disputes; and to become the first president to visit the Alaska Territory. Hoping to reconnect with the American people and put the scandals behind him, Harding called the trip "the Journey of Understanding."

Albert Fall, Harding's secretary of the interior, was convicted of accepting bribes and sentenced to a year in jail and a $100,000 fine.

For two months Harding traveled by train, making speeches and other public appearances in cities and towns all across the country. But no matter how far he traveled, he could not escape the odor of corruption seeping from his administration. Once on the train, he asked Secretary of Commerce Herbert Hoover, "If you knew of a great scandal in our administration, would you for the good of the country and the party expose it publicly or would you bury it?"[48] When Hoover advised him to expose it and asked if Daugherty was involved, Harding changed the subject. His woes weighed on him so heavily that when a ship that he was aboard struck another in a minor accident in Vancouver Harbor, Harding buried his face in his hands and said softly, "I hope the boat sinks."[49]

Complaining of abdominal pain, battling a fever, exhausted, and disheartened, on August 2, 1923, Harding suffered either a cerebral hemorrhage or a massive rupture in the wall of his heart. He died instantly in his room at the Palace Hotel in San Francisco at the age of fifty-seven.

The Teapot Dome Scandal

Although death ended Harding's personal turmoil, it did not quiet allegations of wrongdoing in his administration. Two months after his death, a special Senate committee began public hearings on alleged irregularities in leases for Teapot Dome, a federal military oil reserve in Wyoming. Evidence presented at the hearing revealed that Interior Secretary Fall had been bribed. In exchange for approximately four hundred thousand dollars, Fall had illegally leased not only the Teapot Dome reserve (to oil tycoon Harry F. Sinclair and his Mammoth Oil Company) but also the government's Elk Hills reserve in California (to Edward L. Doheny's Pan American Petroleum and Transport Company). In 1931 Fall became the first cabinet member in history to go to jail for crimes committed while in office.

Daugherty's Turn

At the same time as the Teapot Dome hearings, another Senate committee was investigating Attorney General Daugherty and also looking into Jess Smith's death. A parade of witnesses came forth, telling sensational tales of bribes, kickbacks, and scandalous behavior in a Justice Department run wild. Daugherty refused to cooperate with congressional investigators.

In 1924, President Calvin Coolidge, Harding's successor, forced Daugherty to resign as attorney general. Indicted for conspiracy, Daugherty continually invoked his Fifth Amendment right against self-incrimination during two trials, broadly hinting that he was doing so in order to save Harding's reputation. The ploy had the opposite effect, however, convincing people instead that Harding had somehow been involved in the scandals. This caused the already low opinion that many Americans had of Harding to sink even further. (Daugherty's first trial ended in a hung jury; the second ended with an acquittal due to insufficient evidence.)

Two Best-Sellers

With Harding's reputation already in tatters, in July 1927 Nan Britton published a book called *The President's Daughter*. In it she told the entire story of her illicit love affair with Harding, identifying her daughter Elizabeth Ann as Harding's child.

The President's Daughter rocketed to the top of the best-seller lists, destroying the last remaining shreds of respectability that still clung to Harding's name. Republicans treated the former president as if he had never existed. A special memorial tomb for Harding

A political cartoon lampoons The Teapot Dome Scandal. Bribes were made to get leases for Teapot Dome, a federal military oil reserve.

and his wife (who died in November 1924) was completed in 1927, but no politician would come to Marion to dedicate it. The law school of Ohio Northern University, which had been renamed the Warren G. Harding College of Law in 1921, quietly removed the disgraced president's name.

In 1930 a book called *The Strange Death of President Harding* claimed that Harding had been poisoned by his wife in San Francisco to avoid being impeached and to save his reputation. The public, more than willing to believe anything derogatory about Harding, also turned this book into a best-seller.

A Fitting Epitaph

On June 16, 1931, Republican president Herbert Hoover came to Marion to dedicate Harding's tomb. The United States was mired in the Great Depression, for which Hoover was being blamed. Thus, in one respect, Hoover was as discredited in life as Harding was in death. Perhaps this common bond was what made Hoover speak forcefully and firmly about a president who most Republicans wished had never held the office:

> Warren Harding had a dim realization that he had been betrayed by a few of the men whom he had trusted, by men whom he had believed were his devoted friends. It was later

proved in the courts of the land that these men had betrayed not only the friendship and trust of their staunch and loyal friend but they had betrayed their country.[50]

Hoover's words served as a fitting epitaph for Warren G. Harding. Yet the controversy over his life and his presidency continues. After the president's death, Florence Harding spent five days burning many of his papers, for reasons unknown. In 1964, while doing research in Marion, Harding biographer Francis Russell discovered two hundred love letters from Harding to Carrie Phillips. After a convoluted legal battle between those who wanted the letters to be made public and Harding's heirs and others who opposed such a move, the letters were ordered sealed until the year 2041.

Currently, historians generally agree that Harding was a decent man who was out of his depth in the Oval Office and who was betrayed by those whom he trusted. Perhaps this portrait will change when the sealed letters are finally made public. Almost certainly, the last word has yet to be written about the life of Warren G. Harding and his presidential administration.

CHAPTER 4

Richard M. Nixon

The legacy of Richard M. Nixon's presidency is as mixed as any in U.S. history. Nixon's numerous accomplishments, particularly in foreign policy, could have ranked him as one of the greatest American presidents. During his nearly six years in office, Nixon made important overtures to both China and the Soviet Union. In 1972 he traveled to both the People's Republic of China and the Soviet Union, seeking to thaw the icy relations between the two Communist giants and the United States. The trips resulted in the beginning of dialogues with both countries and helped lessen the threat of nuclear war. In that same year Nixon also signed the Strategic Arms Limitation Treaty with the Soviet Union, which scaled down the military arms race between the two nations. In addition to these achievements, Nixon brought an end to the Vietnam War. His actions resulted in the departure of American troops from Vietnam and the closure of one of the most painfully divisive wars in U.S. history.

Despite these accomplishments, Nixon's legacy is indelibly stained by one of the greatest scandals in presidential history: the Watergate affair. Under the threat of impeachment resulting from his role in the cover-up of the Watergate scandal, Nixon resigned from office. His resignation marked the first time in U.S. history that a chief executive was forced to leave office before the end of his term.

Lemon Groves and Grocery Stores

Richard Milhous Nixon was born on January 9, 1913, in Yorba Linda, California, a small farming community located thirty miles southeast of Los Angeles. His father, Frank Nixon, had moved to California from Ohio to recover from a severe case of frostbite that had occurred while he was working outside in cold weather. In California he met and married a young Quaker named Hannah Milhous. The couple moved to Yorba Linda, where Frank planted a ten-acre grove of lemon trees, hoping to cash in on Southern California's booming citrus industry.

When that endeavor failed, Nixon moved his family to Whittier, California, in 1922 and opened a gas station. Richard, along with his brothers Don and Harold, worked at the station, which

Richard M. Nixon (far right) at the age of three and a half with his father, mother, and two of his brothers.

their father expanded to include a grocery store. Although fond of each other, the three brothers were never close; Richard sought to excel at school, and his devotion to his studies set him apart from the other two. His favorite in the family was his younger brother, Arthur.

The Nixon household was a curious mixture of the quiet, genteel Hannah and the loud, boisterous Frank. Volatile and emotional, Frank Nixon loved a good argument more than anything. He would take whatever side was necessary just to get a debate started—no matter what the subject. Described by one acquaintance as being a man of towering anger, Frank brought these qualities into his home, frequently yelling at his wife and his family and physically striking his children.

Although Hannah never openly criticized her husband, his clamorous behavior bothered her deeply. As was her style, she worked most effectively in the background, quietly seeking ways around his rash disciplinary measures. Yet she was also a stern taskmaster in her own right, and it was her quiet anger, rather than Frank's belligerence, that Richard and the other boys most feared.

Winning Is the Only Thing That Matters

The Nixon household experienced the first in a series of personal tragedies when the youngest son, Arthur, died of tubercular encephalitis in August 1925. Richard, like the rest of the family, was deeply pained by the loss. "For weeks after Arthur's funeral there was not a day that I did not think about him and cry,"[51] Nixon later recalled.

Richard's grief was compounded by the terrible sadness of his parents over the death of their son. Only twelve at the time, he thought he could somehow ease their suffering and make up for his brother's death by devoting himself to his studies and succeeding beyond all expectations at school. Behind this effort was his father's credo that winning (and success) matter most in life. This view lay behind Nixon's actions, both as a young man and also later in life.

Applying himself at school with furious determination, Nixon became president of his eighth-grade class, was voted its outstanding member, and was selected as valedictorian at graduation. In high school Nixon continued to excel academically. He showed a propensity for debating, a skill undoubtedly honed by countless arguments with his opinionated father. In his senior year he unsuccessfully ran for president of his class. The loss, he said later, was his first political defeat.

After graduating from high school third in his class in 1930, Nixon wanted to attend a large, prestigious eastern college. Instead, he wound up enrolling in Whittier College at age seventeen. His older brother Harold had contracted tuberculosis, and between this and a new baby in the family (Edward, born in 1930), Nixon was needed at home to help out.

Yet another tragedy struck the Nixon family in 1933 when Harold died. As before, the loss spurred Richard to greater efforts to ease his parents' grief. According to Hannah Nixon, Harold's death sent Richard "into a deep, impenetrable silence. From that time on, it seemed that he was trying to be three sons in one, striving even harder than before to make up to his father and me for our loss."[52]

At Whittier, Nixon majored in history, became a skilled debater, and was elected freshman class president. In 1934 he graduated second in his class with a B+ average. Nixon accepted a two-hundred-dollar scholarship to Duke University's new law school, and he spent the next three years at Duke in Durham, North Carolina. After graduation he tried but failed to get a job with numerous New York City law firms as well as with the Federal Bureau of Investigation (FBI).

A Return to Whittier

Deeply disappointed by his failure to get a job in the East, Nixon returned to Whittier in the summer of 1937. He passed the California bar exam and then joined a local law firm, primarily practicing estate and divorce law. In 1940 he married schoolteacher Thelma Catherine "Pat" Ryan.

Nixon's California law practice was slow and unexciting. Cases were few, and the work was often tedious. To combat his boredom Nixon plunged into local politics, joining various civic organizations such as the Kiwanis Club.

Nixon soon found another outlet for his pent-up energy. Upon hearing a rumor that the local Republican representative to the California State Assembly might not run again, Nixon began vigorously lobbying for the job, driving across the district on his own time and speaking to small groups. The campaign abruptly stopped when the incumbent decided to run again, but the fledgling effort had accomplished two things: Its conservative message had brought Nixon to the attention of the local Republican organization, and it had established him as an ambitious young man interested in politics.

The First Race

Nixon's political ambitions were put on hold when he entered the U.S. Navy in August 1942. Shortly before his discharge, in September 1945 Nixon's political ambition was remembered when Republicans in California's twelfth congressional district were searching for a candidate to run against popular Democratic incumbent Jerry Voorhis. A campaign against Voorhis, widely considered unbeatable, was going to be as tough as any fight the young naval officer had faced in the military.

"Nobody wanted to run," recalled attorney Stanley Barnes, who turned down an offer to run against Voorhis before Nixon was approached. "They asked a lot of other people to run, but they wouldn't do it."[53]

Nixon, however, would. "I feel very strongly that Jerry Voorhis can be beaten, and I'd welcome the opportunity to take a crack at him,"[54] he said confidently. Although Nixon did receive the nomination, enthusiasm alone would not be enough to unseat Voorhis. The incumbent was so popular and well entrenched that one influential political writer described Nixon's campaign as a lost cause.

Initially, it seemed the pundits were right. Nixon spent most of his time speaking before civic groups, commenting on the evils imposed on the country by the Democrats but including few specifics about his own policies. Then, in April 1946, the flagging campaign got a dramatic boost with the addition of Murray Chotiner.

A fiercely partisan consultant whose ethics had come under fire in some political circles, Chotiner convinced Nixon to drastically escalate his attack on Voorhis by linking him with Communism. This was a surefire attention-getter in the years immediately following

Nixon (top row, fifth from left) with the Duke Law Honor Society in 1937, the year he graduated from law school.

World War II, when the Soviet Union was swallowing up Eastern Europe and Communism seemed poised to dominate the world.

Nixon and Chotiner's attack-dog style of campaigning began to pay off. Newspapers covering the race took notice of Nixon, as did the general public. Nixon's style of public speaking—sharp, short sentences, focused and to the point—was in direct contrast to Voorhis's long-winded, intellectual monologues. Crowds began responding to Nixon and his speeches.

Nixon used various tactics to attract voters, including distorting an opponent's record. Perhaps the most blatant example of this occurred at a public debate, when Nixon criticized Voorhis for having been endorsed by a group called the National Citizens Political Action Committee (NCPAC). At a strategic moment in the debate, Nixon asked Voorhis if he had been endorsed by the PAC-CIO, a labor organization with Communist sympathies. When the congressman denied it, Nixon pulled the NCPAC endorsement from his pocket, announced it to the crowd, and asked Voorhis to look at it. As Nixon had hoped, audience members thought this was the same as an endorsement by the PAC-CIO since the initials were similar, and they began booing Voorhis for trying to hide what they thought was an endorsement by a group with Communist affiliations.

When the congressman tried to redeem himself by mumbling that the two were different groups, Nixon read off the names of people who supposedly served on the boards of both. Then Nixon looked at the audience and said, "It's the same thing, virtually, when they have the same directors."[55] Although this remark was incorrect, the audience again reacted as Nixon had hoped; boos and catcalls rained down on Voorhis.

From that moment, Voorhis was indelibly tarred with the brush of Communism. He could not get rid of the stain for the remainder of the campaign. As Nixon later admitted, "Of course I knew Jerry Voorhis wasn't a Communist. . . . The important thing is to win."[56] Guided by his father's philosophy, Nixon did indeed win, beating Voorhis by over fifteen thousand votes. The politics of dirty tricks had paid its first dividends to Richard Nixon.

The Alger Hiss Case

Nixon entered Congress in January 1947 as part of a historic group of Republican rookies who helped their party take control of both houses of Congress for the first time since 1928. The young congressman's anti-Communist rhetoric had caught the attention of Republican leaders in the House of Representatives, and Nixon was awarded a prestigious committee assignment: a seat on the House

Alger Hiss (right) entering court in New York. Nixon's relentless pursuit of Hiss ended with Hiss being convicted of perjury.

Un-American Activities Committee (HUAC). Republican Party leaders in the House gave the committee the job of eradicating the supposed Communist menace from America.

In another place and another time, Nixon's HUAC assignment might have meant little. But in the late 1940s, Americans were growing increasingly agitated about supposed Soviet infiltration of U.S. society, particularly in light of Soviet takeovers in Eastern Europe. The public wanted any Communists found in American society exposed, and HUAC was only too happy to go looking for them.

Although freshmen congressmen normally do not garner much attention, Nixon was propelled into the national spotlight in August

1948 during the HUAC hearing involving Alger Hiss. Hiss, who had earlier been named as a Communist sympathizer, had compiled an impressive résumé of government service. He had been an aide to Supreme Court justice Oliver Wendell Holmes, an assistant secretary of state in the Roosevelt administration, and secretary-general of the San Francisco Conference, which developed the United Nations charter. At the time of the HUAC hearing, Hiss was president of the prestigious Carnegie Endowment for International Peace.

The idea that such a high-ranking civil servant might be a Communist rattled the country. However, Hiss's testimony before HUAC seemed to disprove the allegations. In fact, Hiss was so successful that people began to feel that the committee's relentless search for Communists in every nook and cranny of American society had gone too far.

"We're ruined,"[57] wailed one of the committee members as HUAC's credibility plunged. Even President Harry Truman joined the chorus of those attacking HUAC by deriding the purpose of the hearings.

But Nixon refused to accept defeat. He continued investigating Hiss's activities and convinced the other committee members to let him head a subcommittee to question Hiss again in secret, without the press and public in attendance.

No one knows what made Nixon insist on continuing the case against Hiss. What is known is that he pursued Hiss with great zeal and was ultimately rewarded when Hiss was convicted of perjury. The conviction rested on statements made by Hiss during the HUAC hearings, including whether he knew the man who accused him of being a Communist. (Hiss served over three years of a five-year prison sentence and was released early in 1954.)

The "Pink Lady"

Nixon emerged from the Hiss hearings as a rising young star in the Republican Party. He easily won re-election in 1948, but it was a bad year for Republicans overall as the Democrats re-took control of Congress. Realizing that his road to leadership in the House would be long and slow, Nixon boldly decided to run for the Senate in 1950 and easily won the Republican primary. When incumbent Democratic senator Sheridan Downey decided not to run, the contest pitted Nixon against Democratic congresswoman Helen Gahagan Douglas, a former Broadway star who had married film actor Melvyn Douglas.

Nixon's Senate campaign made the one against Voorhis look like a model of fair play and good ethics. Sticking to what had worked so well before, Nixon claimed that the liberal Douglas was soft on Communism. He issued a flyer that claimed Douglas had voted with the extremely liberal congressman Vito Marcantonio 353 times. The flyer read, in part,

How can Helen Douglas, capable actress that she is, take up so strange a role as a foe of communism? And why does she when she has so deservedly earned the title of the "pink lady?..." To the communist newspaper the *New York Daily Worker*, Helen Douglas and Vito Marcantonio are heroes.[58]

The Pink Lady label was meant to portray Douglas as a Communist sympathizer since pink is a softer shade of red and the word *red* was commonly used to describe Communists. In reality, the large majority of Douglas's congressional votes that were similar to Marcantonio's were on simple procedural matters that had nothing to do with the safety and security of the United States. In fact, Nixon himself had voted in agreement with Marcantonio 112 times on many of these same matters. But once again, Nixon had used an irrelevant set of similarities to imply sinister intent and play on the emotions of the electorate. The ploy worked. Douglas was branded the Pink Lady, and, like Voorhis before her, could not shake the label. Nixon's anti-Communist rhetoric against Douglas was further boosted by the invasion of U.S.-backed South Korea in June 1950 by Communist North Korea. The war plunged America into an anti-Communist frenzy, and the tide swept Nixon along. He beat Douglas by approximately six hundred thousand votes.

Later, when he was preparing to run for the presidency in 1960 and wanted to appear more moderate, Nixon apologized for the viciousness of the Douglas campaign. "I'm sorry about that episode, I was a very young man,"[59] he told an interviewer in 1958. His apology did little to sway the views of those who were dismayed by his harsh remarks. Nixon's tactics gained him a growing number of political enemies with very long memories, some of whom would plague him throughout his career. "I've never gotten over my hatred of him, really,"[60] said one of Douglas's aides more than twenty-five years later.

Eisenhower's Running Mate

The effects of this, however, were still far in the future. In 1950 Nixon's impressive Senate victory sent his stock soaring in Republican circles. In just five years he had risen from an obscure lawyer to a member of the U.S. Senate, one of the most exclusive and powerful legislative bodies in the world. Any lingering feelings of failure that Nixon still harbored as a result of his return to Whittier after law school must have been washed away by the euphoria of what he had achieved in such a short time.

However, the Senate, like the House, was already proving too stodgy and traditional for Nixon's intense ambition. Thus, in 1952 he accepted the nomination for vice president on the Republican ticket of presidential nominee Dwight D. Eisenhower. The choice seemed logical: Nixon was a young man with a national reputation, and he came from a key state that Eisenhower had to win. In addition, Nixon had legislative knowledge and experience, something that Eisenhower lacked. With the likelihood that the public was ready for a change in the White House after twenty years of Democratic control, it seemed Nixon's climb up the political ladder would continue.

Nixon gave his famous "Checkers" speech to the American people on September 23, 1952.

Checkers

But almost as soon as the campaign began, it was rocked by what has become known as the Checkers scandal. In September 1952 the *New York Post* revealed that Nixon's wealthy California supporters had established a secret campaign fund. The newspaper contended that the $18,000 fund helped Nixon and his family live a lifestyle far above what was possible on his $12,500 Senate salary.

With Eisenhower making an issue of clean government, revelations of the secret fund hurt Republican chances. As the story escalated, Nixon was besieged by advice to resign from the ticket before he dragged down Eisenhower. Harold Stassen, a leading Republican, sent Nixon a model resignation letter. Even Eisenhower seemed to waver in his support, telling reporters, "Of what avail is it for us to carry on this crusade against this business of what has been going on in Washington if we, ourselves, aren't as clean as a hound's tooth?"[61]

With resignation apparently inevitable, Nixon made a last-ditch effort to save both his place on the ticket and his political career. On September 23, 1952, in a televised address to the nation, Nixon made a speech that has become part of American political history. In it he claimed that the money was used to pay political expenses that he did not think should be charged to U.S. taxpayers. To prove that he and his family were not enjoying a luxurious lifestyle and were just scraping along, he listed his various debts and assets, including his wife's dowdy coat, saying, "I should say this, that Pat doesn't have a mink coat. But she does have a respectable cloth coat. And I always tell her that she'd look good in anything."[62]

Then, having established himself as a victim of persecution by his political enemies, Nixon went for the emotional jugular of his audience. He related how he and his family did, indeed, receive one gift from a political supporter:

> It was a little cocker spaniel dog in a crate that he sent all the way from Texas. Black and white spotted. And our little girl—Tricia, the six-year-old, named it Checkers. And you know the kids love the dog and I just want to say this right now, that regardless of what they say about it, we're gonna keep it.[63]

Although Nixon closed the speech by asking the public to decide whether he should remain on the ticket, the question was unnecessary. His emotional appeal had won the day. Expressions of support poured into Republican National Committee headquarters at a rate of 350 to 1 in Nixon's favor. The young senator remained on the ticket and became vice president when Eisenhower swept to victory in November.

Defeats and a Comeback

Nixon served eight years as vice president. In 1960 the Republican Party nominated him to run for president against Democratic senator John F. Kennedy from Massachusetts. In one of the closest presidential elections in American history, Kennedy beat Nixon by approximately 112,000 popular votes. Kennedy's victory was credited in large part to his performance in a series of televised debates against Nixon. In particular, during the first debate the tanned, confident Kennedy projected a much more appealing image than the nervous, somber-looking Nixon.

After this defeat, Nixon's political career faltered. In 1962 he lost badly in a race for the California governor's office. The morning after the election, he blasted members of the media (whom he blamed for unfair press coverage during the campaign) at a press conference, telling them, "Just think how much you're going to be missing. You won't have Nixon to kick around anymore, because, gentlemen, this is my last press conference."[64]

After that spiteful session, most political observers considered Nixon's political career finished. But a series of events that no one could have foreseen completely reorganized the political landscape. It began in 1963, when the assassination of President Kennedy put Vice President Lyndon Johnson in the Oval Office. Johnson's landslide victory over Republican senator Barry Goldwater in the 1964 presidential election left the Republican Party in disarray. Nixon saw an opportunity to move into the leadership vacuum left by Goldwater's stinging defeat. He spoke out frequently on domestic and foreign policy issues, and in 1966 he campaigned for Republican congressional candidates.

By 1968 protests over the Vietnam War and riots in American cities led the beleaguered Johnson to decline renomination, and the Democrats subsequently picked his vice president, Hubert Humphrey, as their presidential candidate. The Republicans chose Nixon; by now his political views had moderated, and he seemed like a good compromise between the party's liberal and conservative wings. In addition, many party members were grateful for his past efforts on behalf of Republican candidates.

The presidential election that autumn was extremely close. However, Nixon prevailed. In January 1969, Nixon took office as the thirty-seventh president of the United States.

President Richard Nixon shakes hands with Vice President Spiro Agnew after taking the oath of office.

President Nixon

Nixon's election did not calm American anxiety about the Vietnam War, race riots, antiwar protests, and the assassinations of John F. Kennedy, Robert Kennedy, and Martin Luther King. The Vietnam War dragged on. In fact, when the United States began bombing Communist supply bases in Cambodia in April 1970, it seemed to many that the war was escalating, not winding down. In a tragic showdown, students at Kent State University in Ohio who protested the Cambodian invasion were fired on by National Guard troops on May 4. Four students were killed, further traumatizing the country.

Although victory eluded America, Nixon managed to gradually withdraw American troops via a policy called Vietnamization, which shifted the military burden to America's South Vietnamese allies. This policy as well as his foreign policy initiatives to the Soviet Union and China were positive developments that fueled voter support for Nixon. On November 7, 1972, Nixon was reelected president, winning forty-nine of fifty states in a landslide victory over Democratic candidate George McGovern.

This was Nixon's greatest political triumph—an overwhelming electoral victory that gave him an undeniable mandate from the American people. Yet the victory brought Nixon little satisfaction. The Democrats stayed in control of both houses of Congress, the antiwar movement remained a potent force, and his political foes were still waiting for an opportunity to strike. Instead of reveling in his win, Nixon was morose and gloomy, dwelling on the difficult road ahead. As historian Stephen E. Ambrose writes,

> So, on election night 1972, Nixon could not enjoy his triumph. He was not planning how to bring people together, to create a consensus behind his program, but rather how to destroy his enemies before they destroyed him. In his own immortal phrase, "They are asking for it, and they are going to get it."[65]

Ambrose reports that in a staff meeting the next day, National Security Adviser Henry Kissinger found Nixon to be "grim and remote." "It was as if victory was not an occasion for reconciliation but an opportunity to settle the scores of a lifetime,"[66] Kissinger later recalled.

Watergate

One of the things that might have weighed on the president's mind was an incident that had begun during the 1972 campaign. In the early morning hours of June 17, five men dressed in business suits had been arrested in the act of breaking into the headquarters of the Democratic National Committee, which was located in the Watergate building complex in Washington, D.C. It was soon revealed that the men had intended to plant electronic listening devices in the Democratic headquarters as well as engage in other forms of political espionage.

Although one of the men arrested was working for the Committee to Re-elect the President and the Republican National Committee, the operation at first was viewed as just a bungled burglary aimed at acquiring sensitive campaign information. It was assumed that the men arrested were merely overzealous political operatives with no expertise in the techniques of petty crime.

But the Watergate break-in was just the tip of the iceberg. As time passed, the true dimensions of an elaborate and sophisticated scheme of political espionage became clear. What had seemed initially like a minor burglary was found to be part of a master plan by the Nixon administration to punish its enemies through whatever means—legal or otherwise—possible. Nixon was making good on his threat to wreak vengeance on his political enemies.

Although Nixon did not know about the Watergate break-in ahead of time, he immediately ordered a cover-up to protect himself once the break-in became public knowledge. Long accustomed to manipulating the truth and denying accountability, such as in his campaigns against Voorhis and Douglas, Nixon reverted to these techniques in the Watergate scandal, hoping that the strategy that had worked so well previously would work again.

The Watergate Hotel complex, headquarters of the Democratic National Committee and scene of the infamous break-in.

The Noose Tightens

But he miscalculated. As investigators and reporters began uncovering the tangled web of events connected to the break-in, Nixon found himself more and more at risk and took even more desperate measures to save himself. When he attempted to have the Central Intelligence Agency (CIA) block an FBI investigation into the break-in, it was an abuse of presidential powers. When information came out about a dirty-tricks unit of the White House known as the Plumbers, which performed political espionage on Nixon's enemies (such as spreading false and damaging rumors about Democratic candidates), the president blamed several members of his staff and fired them. When a special prosecutor appointed to investigate Watergate (as the entire scandal came to be called) demanded White House tape recordings that Nixon knew would reveal his knowledge of the cover-up, he ordered the attorney general to fire the prosecutor. When the attorney general refused, the president fired him and also the deputy attorney general when he refused a similar order. Finally, the solicitor general carried out Nixon's demand. (However, the outcry over this action was so intense that Nixon was forced to appoint another special prosecutor.)

As the investigative trail drew closer and closer to the Oval Office, Nixon grew frantic to save his presidency. "I don't give a s—— what happens, I want you all to stonewall it, let them [the Watergate defendants] plead the Fifth Amendment, cover-up, or anything else, if it'll save it, save the plan,"[67] he said to one of his subordinates.

But there was no saving the plan. Little by little, the cover-up crumbled as numerous administration officials were found to be involved in Watergate. Nixon's public support steadily eroded as more and more evidence emerged concerning the sordid Watergate affair.

While Watergate was unfolding, yet another scandal emerged within the Nixon administration, this one concerning Vice President Spiro Agnew. On October 9, 1973, Agnew resigned after pleading nolo contendere (no contest) to one count of having knowingly failed to report income for tax purposes. He received three years probation and a ten thousand dollar fine. Congressional minority leader Gerald Ford was selected to replace Agnew.

Resignation

But Watergate overshadowed even the extraordinary event of a vice presidential resignation. By 1974 twenty-nine people had been indicted, had pled guilty, or had been convicted of Watergate-related

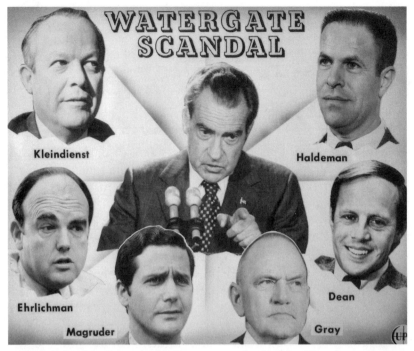

Nixon and six staff members who were involved in the Watergate cover-up. All were forced to resign.

crimes. By early August of that year, deprived of his key advisers, virtually devoid of both public and political support, and facing almost certain impeachment in the House and conviction by the Senate, Nixon was forced to confront the harsh reality of his situation. On August 8, 1974, he resigned from office.

The president of the United States had been brought down by what his press secretary had once scornfully dismissed as a third-rate burglary. In September 1974, President Gerald Ford pardoned Nixon for any crimes he might have committed. The pardon generated a huge amount of controversy, and some historians believe it cost Ford the 1976 presidential election.

In the years immediately following Watergate, Nixon was a political pariah, shunned by members of both parties. Gradually, however, he reemerged in the public eye, writing books on America's role in the world and becoming an elder statesman on the U.S. political scene. When Nixon died on April 22, 1994, there was an outpouring of public sympathy for him as people chose to remember his diplomatic breakthroughs and his success at ending the Vietnam War. These triumphs will always be counterbalanced, however, by the foul legacy of Watergate.

CHAPTER 5

Ronald Reagan

Ronald Reagan became the fortieth president of the United States at a critical juncture in American history. At the time of his election, the United States was reeling from numerous domestic and foreign crises that had sapped the nation's spirit. At home, runaway inflation combined with an energy shortage had sent shock waves through America's economy. Abroad, the rise in international terrorism and the inability to free fifty-three American hostages held captive by Iranian radicals made the United States seem helpless in world affairs. In the midst of these events, Americans questioned themselves, their leaders, and the direction of their country.

Reagan changed all that. His confident nature and friendly smile were a perfect antidote to an American public grown weary of the secretive presidency of Richard Nixon and the indecisiveness of Jimmy Carter. Domestically, Reagan's tax cuts made Americans feel that the economy was improving and that they had more money to spend. On the international scene, Reagan's unhesitating use of U.S. military power to combat terrorism and aggression restored American confidence in the nation's ability to control its own destiny and assume an important role in world affairs.

Reagan's popularity with the electorate remained high—high enough to win him two terms in office. During that time, Reagan's honesty and integrity were seldom questioned. Not so the members of his administration, however. By the end of Reagan's second term more than two hundred of his appointees were facing allegations of ethical or criminal wrongdoing. And, although the honesty of the president was never in question, one of the scandals —the Iran-Contra affair—was so serious that some of Reagan's aides feared his impeachment.

Born in a Blizzard

Ronald Wilson Reagan was born during a howling blizzard on February 6, 1911, in the tiny town of Tampico, Illinois (population 1,276). His father, Jack Reagan, was an alcoholic shoe salesman who stumbled from one low-paying job to another, always searching for his big break. By the time Ronald was nine years old, the family had already moved four times. Ronald's mother, Nelle, was a kind, energetic woman who was always doing good deeds for others, whether it was visiting hospital patients or donating food to the less fortunate.

Despite his alcoholism, Jack Reagan instilled in his son core values that shaped his life and formed the foundation of his political philosophy: "My father believed energy and hard work were the only ingredients needed for success,"[68] Reagan later said. Although the elder Reagan's perpetual search for his own personal pot of gold led to frequent disappointments, Ronald grew up to be an optimist, always certain that something wonderful lay around the next corner.

Reagan was a good student in school, but his true passion was sports. His heroes were the mythic athletes of the age, such as New York Yankee outfielder Babe Ruth and boxing great Jack Dempsey. His favorite sport, however, was football, and his passion for the game lasted his entire life.

After graduating high school Reagan attended Eureka College in Eureka, Illinois, on an athletic scholarship. There, he pursued his dream of becoming an All-American football player, although his desire was stronger than his talent and he was never able to play up to that level.

During his freshman year the sports-loving Reagan discovered a new passion when he went to see a touring London play called *Journey's End*. Something about the play and its main character reached deep into the heart of the young college student. By the time the performance was over, the acting bug had bitten Reagan.

Sports Announcer

However, acting was not considered a legitimate career at that time, so upon graduation from college in June 1932, Reagan sought employment in other professions. He could not have picked a worse time to be seeking a job; the Great Depression was at its zenith,

Ronald Reagan, fortieth president of the United States.

Ronald Reagan began his career as a sports broadcaster on WOC radio in Davenport, Iowa.

and almost 12 million Americans were out of work. But thanks to his knowledge of football, the affable Reagan talked himself into a job announcing University of Iowa football games. By the beginning of 1933 he was working as a staff announcer at radio station WOC in Davenport, Iowa. At a time of economic upheaval, when a machinist in Iowa earned 63¢ per hour and a telephone company technician made $16.36 per week, Reagan's salary was a princely $100 per month.

Although he knew virtually nothing about broadcasting, Reagan's natural warmth and personality came through over the radio. He was also blessed with a clear, pleasant voice that could be mellow and persuasive when necessary, drawing listeners in with its straightforward charm and sense of intimacy. As one observer said, "He likes his voice, treats it like a guest. He makes you part of the hospitality."[69]

When he was transferred to WOC's sister station, WHO, in Des Moines, Reagan added re-creations of Chicago Cub baseball games to his on-air repertoire. In the days before television, many announcers at small radio stations received pitch-by-pitch accounts of baseball games via telegraph and then pretended that they were actually at the stadium, calling the action as it happened and describing the sights and sounds of a major league game. Game re-creation was a highly sought-after skill among sports announcers, and Reagan was one of the best at it, thanks to his smooth voice and quick wit. Once during a game, the telegraph wire went dead, leaving Reagan with nothing to report to his audience. Thinking quickly, he had the batter foul off pitch after pitch until service was restored.

The Silver Screen Beckons

Despite his success as a sports announcer, Reagan never forgot his dream of acting. Early in 1937 he talked WHO into sending him to Catalina, California, to cover the Cubs at spring training. While in Southern California, he wangled a screen test at Warner Brothers. Despite his own feeling that he was "terrible," the studio saw enough promise in the handsome young man with the great voice to sign him to a contract at two hundred dollars per week.

At Warner's Reagan became a mainstay of the company's "B" pictures (movies made quickly and cheaply without the production values and stars of "A" films). He appeared in sixteen films between 1938 and 1939. His big break came in the 1940 film *Knute Rockne—All American*, the story of the legendary Notre Dame football coach. Reagan played George Gipp, a Notre Dame player who, while dying of pneumonia, implored Rockne to have the team "win one for the Gipper." Although it was a small role, Reagan drew on his football experience to give a powerful performance. This led to parts in better pictures, allowing him to shed his image as a "B" film actor.

Reagan's personal life was enjoying a similar upturn. In 1940 he married actress Jane Wyman, and for a time the attractive couple were the darlings of Hollywood.

But then things changed for Reagan. After the United States entered World War II, he was called to active duty in the armed forces in April 1942. Too nearsighted to be assigned to a fighting unit, Reagan spent his time in the military in the First Motion Picture Unit of the U.S. Army Air Corps, acting in training films. By the time he was discharged from the military late in 1945, there was a new generation of moviegoers who barely knew the name Ronald Reagan.

Reagan's normally sunny disposition, already clouded by his career woes, took a further hit in 1947, when he was stricken with viral pneumonia and nearly died. The following year his eight-year marriage to Wyman collapsed (they were divorced in 1949), sending Reagan into a deep depression.

With his marriage over and his career in shambles, Reagan, still under contract to Warner Brothers, began lobbying the studio for the right to appear in better pictures than those they had chosen for him. When Warner's rejected his efforts, Reagan renegotiated his contract to allow him to become a freelance actor and get out from under the studio's control over his roles. He made fifteen films between 1947 and 1952 for various studios, including one that ranks among his best: *The Winning Team*, about the great yet troubled pitcher Grover Cleveland Alexander.

Just as his film career rebounded, so did his personal life. On March 4, 1952, he married actress Nancy Davis, who gave up her career to become a wife and mother. The couple had two children, Patricia and Ronald.

A New Career

Although Reagan now had more control over his film career, his interest in movies waned during the 1950s. Instead, he focused his energies on two other areas: television and labor relations. In 1947 he had been elected president of the Screen Actors Guild (SAG), the union that represents actors and actresses in the motion picture industry.

Reagan's labor activism went hand in hand with his own experiences at Warner Brothers and with his political views. Reagan favored the Democratic Party's support for workers and labor unions and supported its battle for higher wages and better benefits for working men and women.

But in 1954 an event occurred in Reagan's life that had a profound effect on his political views: He was hired as host of *General Electric Theatre*, a television program sponsored by one of America's biggest corporations. As part of his contract, he had to tour the United States, plugging the company's products and meeting its employees. Through his friendly relationship with General Electric (GE), Reagan came to view big business in a more favorable light than before, particularly during his dealings with Warner Brothers. When GE executives complained about government regulations that they felt were hampering their business, they found a sympathetic audience in Reagan.

At the same time, his work for GE had caused his income to rise. He felt that the government was taking far too much money out of his wages for taxes and that government in general had become bloated and intrusive. Ultimately, his new outlook on big business and government merged, changing his political philosophy from liberal to conservative. Before long, the faithful Democrat was sounding the call of the Republicans. His speeches had titles such as "Our Eroding Freedoms," and in them he attacked big government and wasteful spending.

Despite his changing views, Reagan still considered himself a Democrat. That changed early in 1961, when Democrat John F. Kennedy was inaugurated as president. That same week Reagan gave his standard evils-of-big-government speech, only to be attacked by a pro-labor newspaper as a right-wing extremist. The former labor activist was stunned. "I'd been making this same speech for years, and no one objected," Reagan said, "and a Democratic President is elected and suddenly they find I'm a right-wing extremist."[70] One year later Reagan officially changed his political affiliation to Republican.

Reagan (top) with other screen stars at a meeting of the Screen Actors Guild (SAG). He was elected president of SAG in 1947.

Throughout most of his life good fortune had smiled on Ronald Reagan, and the birth of his political career was no exception. In 1964 he gave a televised speech in support of conservative Republican presidential candidate Barry Goldwater. The speech was one of the few highlights of the Arizona senator's dismal campaign. Goldwater's crushing defeat by Democrat Lyndon Johnson left the conservative faction of the party leaderless—a power vacuum that Reagan easily filled.

Two years later it was Johnson who was on the defensive. The escalating war in Vietnam and doubts about Johnson's Great Society social programs (which provided government assistance to poor and middle-class Americans) were cutting into support of the Democratic Party. Reagan's conservative, antigovernment philosophy became more and more popular.

California Governor

In 1966 the Republican Party in California nominated Reagan to run for governor. His opponent was incumbent Democrat Edmund G. "Pat" Brown, who had amassed an impressive record of accomplishment. California had both a highway network and a parks system that was the envy of the nation, as well as an excellent state university system and a vigorous program of college construction.

An experienced politician, Brown took the newcomer Reagan lightly and ran a poor campaign. One of Brown's worst moments came in a television commercial, when he told a group of schoolchildren, "I'm running against an actor, and you know who shot Lincoln, don't 'cha?"[71] He also failed to listen to the voters, who, buffeted by inflation and trying to raise families, wanted lower taxes, not more government programs and higher taxes to pay for them. On Election Day, Reagan beat Brown by nearly 1 million votes.

Reagan served two terms as California's governor. The experience was an eye-opener for him. He quickly discovered that it was one thing to campaign on popular ideas like cutting taxes, but it was another thing to actually implement a tax cut because such a move usually required painful program and spending cuts.

Running California was literally on-the-job training for Reagan. Except for his SAG days, he had no experience either in politics or with entrenched bureaucracies. Reagan found that he was good at presenting aides and the public with a broad picture of his views and ideals. He left it to staff members to work out the details since he had no interest in that aspect of public policy. As governor, Reagan helped reform the state's welfare system, slowed

Ronald Reagan as governor of California in 1966.

the growth of the state workforce by imposing a temporary hiring freeze, and also enacted a tax rebate program.

By 1974, after two terms as California governor, Reagan stepped aside, despite the urging of aides and friends to run for a third term. These were dark days for Republicans, with President Richard Nixon besieged by the Watergate scandal and the party's stock plummeting among voters. Many Republicans believed that Reagan, unsullied by Watergate, could repair their party's damaged image.

Running for President

In November 1975 Reagan announced his candidacy for the Republican presidential nomination, placing himself in direct competition with President Gerald Ford, who had taken over after Nixon's resignation. This surprised many Reagan supporters, who knew that he had long preached what he called the Eleventh Commandment: Thou shalt not criticize another Republican. Reagan had convinced himself that his campaign would not be divisive for the party, but as Ford would later say, "How can you challenge an incumbent president of your own party and *not* be divisive?"[72]

The fight for the Republican presidential nomination was indeed bitter. It carried all the way to the party's nominating convention in Kansas City in the summer of 1976. There, in an exceptionally close race, Ford won the nomination by the narrow margin of 117 votes.

"Don't get cynical," Reagan told his followers in defeat. "Lay me down and bleed awhile. Though I am wounded, I am not slain. I shall rise and fight again."[73]

And rise again he did, four years later. Ford's loss to Jimmy Carter in 1976 (which he blamed on Reagan's primary challenge) left the Republican field wide open. Building on his name recognition and the strength he had shown in 1976, Reagan swept to victory in the presidential primaries and gained the nomination on the first ballot at the Republican convention. His opponent in the November election was President Carter.

Normally it is difficult to challenge an incumbent president, who can use the power of the office to garner free publicity and get his message out to the voters while not appearing to be campaigning. But Carter was weakened by rampant inflation and his inability to free fifty-three Americans taken hostage by terrorists in Iran. Many people felt that the country was drifting and needed stronger leadership in both domestic and foreign affairs.

Reagan framed the election in simple yet effective terms by asking voters if they were better off than they had been before Carter became president. On Election Day the voters answered the question: Reagan swamped Carter, winning 50 percent of the popular vote to 41 percent for the president. When he was inaugurated in January 1981, Reagan was sixty-nine years old; only the ninth president of the United States, William Henry Harrison, had been older.

A Relaxed Style

Reagan brought the same relaxed management style to the presidency that he had used as California's governor. He expounded on ideals and principles but delegated policy and practical matters to staffers and aides. Reagan scorned the idea of working long hours, as some of his predecessors had done, preferring a nine to five routine whenever possible. "Show me an executive who works long overtime hours and I'll show you a bad executive,"[74] he said. During the campaign, after complaining to an aide that his schedule had forced him to get up too early that morning, the aide replied that he had better get used to it, for if he became president, a National Security Council official would be waiting to brief him everyday at 7:30. "Well," shot back Reagan, "he's going to have a helluva long wait."[75]

Such folksy stories about Reagan, along with his easygoing personality and his natural friendliness, helped fuel public affection for him. This affection increased dramatically after Reagan was wounded on March 30, 1981, in an assassination attempt. Quipping that he forgot to duck, Reagan showed the country that not even a would-be assassin's bullet could alter his sunny disposition.

Chairman of the Board

Although his personality seemed well suited to the presidency, Reagan's management style soon plunged his administration into trouble. As biographer Lou Cannon writes, Reagan saw himself as "the chairman of the board of a great corporation," and a chairman does not get involved in day-to-day details. As Cannon notes, "By temperament and training, Reagan simply was not a detail man."[76] This left much of the actual work up to his subordinates.

Many of these people did not merit the trust he placed in them. Reagan appointed people to government jobs without considering their qualifications or knowing whether they were suitable. As Haynes Johnson writes in *Sleepwalking Through History*, "He [Reagan] seemed to take it for granted that he could appoint people of dubious qualification and expect that government would work well."[77]

By 1988, at the end of Reagan's second term in office, his administration was awash in scandal. Among those affected were Labor Secretary Raymond Donovan, White House chief of staff Michael Deaver, Attorney General Edwin Meese, various government agencies, and an assortment of federal, state, and local Republican appointees.

The Environmental Protection Agency (EPA) was one of the federal departments hit hardest by scandal. In October 1982 the House of Representatives launched an investigation of the EPA's toxic waste cleanup program. However, Reagan ordered EPA administrator Anne Gorsuch (her name was changed to Anne Burford when she remarried in February 1983) to withhold some of the documents that the House's investigating agencies wanted to subpoena. Because of this, the House voted in December 1982 to cite Gorsuch for contempt of Congress. The House did not receive the documents until months later.

Much of the investigation focused on the EPA's solid waste division and its head, Assistant Administrator Rita M. Lavelle. She was charged with displaying favoritism toward some companies with whom she discussed pending EPA enforcement actions. There were also accusations of misuse of funds

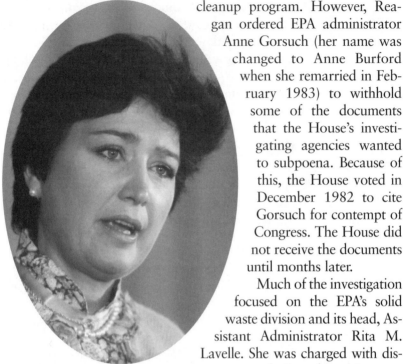

EPA administrator Anne Burford resigned in March 1983 following accusations of misusing funds.

dedicated to cleaning up toxic waste sites. Reagan was forced to dismiss Lavelle in February 1983 after she had refused Burford's request to resign. Lavelle was found guilty of perjury before Congress and served three months in jail. Burford resigned in March, leaving behind a discredited agency with sagging morale. More than twenty EPA officials had resigned by the autumn of 1983.

Supply-Side Scandals

The traditional view of public office—as a means of serving the public—seemed to lose ground during the years of Reagan's presidency. Public office, some observers say, was seen instead as an avenue to acquisition of wealth and personal gain. This mindset had unfortunate results. As Johnson notes, "The Reagan years were marked by numerous instances of officials cashing in on their public positions for personal profit."[78] Reagan-appointed officials in over one dozen federal agencies, including the Postal Service, the Agriculture Department, the Veterans Administration, the

Transportation Department, and the Social Security Agency, took advantage of the very federal programs that they were supposed to be administering.

The prevailing mood among many Reagan appointees could be summed up in the words of former agriculture secretary John Block. When asked by the *Wall Street Journal* why he had applied for federal aid for his own farm when he had been advocating cutting farm subsidies, Block said, "If they're going to shower all this money around, we're going to get some of it."[79]

Scandals involving presidential appointees and federal agencies, although a negative mark against the administration, did not directly impact the president. However, two years after being overwhelmingly reelected to a second term, a major scandal did affect Reagan—a scandal so serious that some of his aides worried that it could lead to impeachment.

The Iran-Contra Affair

In early November 1986 a magazine based in Beirut, Lebanon, called *Al Shiraa* revealed that, for the past year, the CIA had secretly sold weapons to Iran, a country that supported anti-American terrorism and was fighting a war with Iraq. In exchange, Iran had used its influence to secure the release of two Americans who were being held hostage by a pro-Iranian group in Lebanon called Hezbollah ("Party of God").

The news was astounding because Reagan had repeatedly vowed that the United States would not negotiate with terrorists or nations like Iran that supported terrorism. Additionally, the article suggested that the United States was negotiating with terrorists by trading weapons for hostages.

But in the president's opinion, there had been no negotiation:

> The terrorists have not profited. We let the Iranians buy the supplies and they influenced the terrorists. There were no benefits to the terrorists. We are working with moderates, hoping in the future to be able to influence Iran after [dictatorial Iranian leader Ayatollah Ruhollah] Khomeini dies.[80]

Learning of the deal, some of Reagan's aides pointed out that arms sales to Iran violated two U.S. laws: One banned military sales to Iran because of its support for terrorism while the other required that Congress receive "timely" notice of any CIA covert activity in the name of national security. Yet the administration had not notified Congress of the Iranian operation.

New Details Emerge

The story grew more complex and more troubling when it was further revealed that between $10 and $30 million of the profits from the Iranian arms sales had been diverted by some members of the administration's National Security Council to help support the Contras, resistance fighters trying to oust Nicaragua's elected leftist government. Reagan enthusiastically supported the Contras and their mission, but Congress had eliminated their funding in October 1984. If the president had knowingly approved the diversion of funds to the Contras, he would have been guilty of vi-

President Reagan admits in a television address to the American people that arms were traded for hostages, and the profits funneled to Nicaraguan Contras.

Admiral John Poindexter (left) and Lieutenant Colonel Oliver North testify before a house committee on the Iran-Contra Affair.

olating the will of Congress—a charge with the potential to bring down the entire administration. As former *Washington Post* reporter Bob Woodward writes in *Shadow*, "Discussions of impeachment were nearly everywhere in Washington."[81]

Iran-Contra mushroomed into the biggest presidential scandal since Watergate. A special prosecutor was named to investigate the entire affair, and Congress held hearings. Throughout it all, Reagan insisted that he was unaware of the diversion of funds to the Contras and that his national security advisers had acted without his approval. "I didn't know anything about it," Reagan said. "They never mentioned to me any diversion of funds."[82]

It was never proved that the president knew about the funds being sent to the Contras. Admiral John Poindexter, the president's national security adviser, and Lieutenant Colonel Oliver North, an aide to the National Security Council, testified before Congress that they had never told Reagan about the illegal operation. When told of Poindexter's testimony, Reagan laughed. "See. I've been saying the same thing for seven months. What was everyone worried about?"[83]

Despite his testimony exonerating the president, North was convicted of falsifying and destroying documents, accepting an illegal gratuity, and aiding and abetting the obstruction of Congress. Poindexter was found guilty of five criminal counts. Both men's convictions were later overturned on technical grounds.

The Effects of Iran-Contra

Although investigators cleared the president, the Iran-Contra scandal threw a pall over the last years of the Reagan presidency. A report issued in 1987 by a commission investigating the scandal criticized Reagan and his advisers for letting the National Security Council run wild. The deficiencies of Reagan's relaxed management style were exposed before the entire country, and many people were shocked because the president seemed to be out of touch with events. The scandal altered Reagan's image from that of a forceful leader to someone who did not know what was happening within his own administration.

Even after Reagan left the White House, scandals linked to his administration continued to be unearthed. In the spring of 1989, just three months into the presidency of George Bush, word leaked of massive abuse and mismanagement at the Department of Housing and Urban Development (HUD). Haynes Johnson summarizes the content of these leaks:

> HUD became the personal vehicle for the rich and politically well connected to exploit low-income housing programs designed to help the poor. Dozens of former officials, many from HUD and others with close ties to the Reagan White House, earned millions of dollars in consulting fees in return for their efforts in winning HUD housing subsidies and grants for their clients. Many of these people had no background or expertise in housing; their reward was based solely on high political connections.[84]

Ronald Reagan came into the White House with the reputation as a tough leader and the hope that he would reenergize the American spirit. He certainly accomplished the second goal; by the end of his presidency Americans once again felt confident about their country and its future. This was due in large part to Reagan's unflappable optimism in the strength of the United States and his belief that it was a nation destined for greatness.

Despite numerous scandals involving members of his administration, Reagan's personal popularity remained high throughout his two terms of office. Even after he left the White House, Reagan was a beloved figure, and millions of Americans were saddened in November 1994 when he announced that he was suffering from Alzheimer's disease.

However, the scandals did tarnish his legacy and the reputation of his administration. Iran-Contra also altered his personal image; reports suggesting that he did not know what was going on in the White House softened his rough-and-ready, cowboy image to that of a kindly grandfather, sitting idly by while his grandchildren ran roughshod about his home. How history will ultimately view the presidency of Ronald Reagan is still uncertain.

CHAPTER 6

Bill Clinton

President Bill Clinton, America's forty-second president, was the first Democratic president to be elected to two consecutive terms since Franklin D. Roosevelt sixty years earlier. During Clinton's eight years in office, America experienced vigorous economic growth and the rise of electronic commerce. A balanced budget and peace initiatives in Northern Ireland and the Middle East were among the Clinton administration's numerous other accomplishments.

Yet over everything looms the shadow of impeachment. In December 1998 Clinton became only the second president in U.S. history to be impeached by the Congress (Andrew Johnson was the first), and the first elected president to have that judgment passed on him. He was elected to his first term in 1992, the first U.S. president born after World War II, a young man to lead America into the twenty-first century. Instead, the promise of the Clinton presidency dissolved in the midst of one of the worst scandals ever to strike the nation's highest office.

Ironically, it was events that occurred before Clinton even became president—a charge that he sexually harassed a woman when he was the governor of Arkansas—that triggered the scandal that ultimately led to his impeachment. Accusations of womanizing and infidelity had dogged Clinton repeatedly throughout his career and possibly even kept him from making an earlier run for the presidency. Although he had always been able to overcome such allegations before, he could not beat them back this time and was forced to endure the agony of impeachment.

Early Adversity

On May 17, 1946, three months before the future president was born, his father, William Jefferson Blythe, was killed in an automobile accident. Virginia Blythe named her baby, born on August 19, 1946, William Jefferson "Bill" Blythe III.

For the first few years of his life, Bill lived with his grandparents in Hope, Arkansas, while his mother was away in New Orleans studying to become a nurse-anesthetist. During this time Virginia Blythe began dating Roger Clinton, who ran a Buick automobile dealership in Hope, and on June 19, 1950, the two were married. An alcoholic, Clinton was abusive toward his family, and this behavior forced his stepson to act as protector for his mother and half brother, Roger (born when Bill was ten years old).

Although Bill's relationship with his stepfather was stormy, at age fifteen he legally took the Clinton name in order to share the same last name as Roger. As he grew older Bill Clinton made peace with his stepfather. When Roger Clinton was dying of cancer in 1967, Bill helped him maintain his dignity and quality of life as much as possible during the last months of his illness.

In school Clinton was a dedicated student with a yen for music. He played the saxophone and formed a three-piece jazz band called Three Blind Mice. In the summer of 1963 Clinton participated in Boys State, a program in which students study politics. Clinton later traveled to Washington, D.C., as a delegate to the national program called Boys Nation. It was on this trip that he met his hero, President John F. Kennedy, and shook his hand. That meeting, at age seventeen,

Seventeen-year-old Bill Clinton shakes hands with President Kennedy at the White House. This meeting inspired Clinton to pursue a life of politics.

changed Clinton's life. Because of it he decided that he too would go into politics.

After graduating from high school Clinton entered Georgetown University in Washington, D.C., in the autumn of 1964 to study international affairs. Although many students are uncertain of their career path when they first attend college, Clinton already had his sights set on a political future. "Bill became involved in politics right away," said Tom Campbell, Clinton's Georgetown roommate. "He was very focused on where he was and what he wanted to do."[85]

Trying to soak up as much on-the-job political training as possible, Clinton, during his summer vacation one year, worked for Arkansas gubernatorial candidate Frank Holt. Although Holt lost, his nephew (an Arkansas Supreme Court justice) was impressed enough by Clinton to get him a job in the Washington, D.C., office of Arkansas senator J. William Fulbright.

Vietnam and the Draft

In 1968, at age twenty-two, Clinton graduated from Georgetown and was awarded a prestigious Rhodes Scholarship to Oxford University in England. That same year, hundreds of thousands of U.S. soldiers were being sent to fight in Vietnam. Like many other college students of his generation, Clinton elected to continue his education rather than go to war. During his first year at Oxford, where he was studying for a bachelor of philosophy in politics, Clinton was called to active duty in the U.S. military, but he obtained a student deferment that allowed him to complete the school year. He then got the draft notice canceled by agreeing to join the Reserve Officers' Training Corps (ROTC) program at the University of Arkansas Law School.

But instead of returning to Arkansas, he decided to return to Oxford for a second year, and so once again became eligible for the draft. However, by this time a lottery system based on a random drawing of birth dates was being used to select draftees. Clinton's birth date was not one of those chosen, and so he was not drafted. Clinton's draft deferment would come back to haunt him during his presidential campaigns and throughout his terms in office. Opponents charged him with being a draft dodger unfit to lead the nation's armed forces.

Clinton left Oxford after his second year, without getting a degree, to accept a scholarship to Yale's law school in New Haven, Connecticut. There he met Hillary Rodham, a fellow student also interested in politics and the law. In 1972 they both worked on the presidential campaign of Democratic senator George McGovern, and in 1975 they were married.

The First Foray into Politics

After graduating from Yale, Clinton accepted a teaching position at the law school of the University of Arkansas and seemed poised for a life in academia. But the political urge was too strong for him to resist. Early in 1974 Clinton decided to run for Congress against John Paul Hammerschmidt, the popular Republican incumbent in Arkansas's third congressional district. Although not given much of a chance, Clinton drew on his previous political experience to run a determined, effective campaign that came within six thousand votes of defeating Hammerschmidt. The campaign marked Bill Clinton as a rising star among Arkansas Democrats.

In 1976 Clinton ran for Arkansas attorney general. His opponent in the Democratic primary, George Jernigan, was stunned by the young man's political savvy. "He's the best campaigner I've ever seen," Jernigan later said. "Clinton had spent the two years since he had been defeated [in the congressional race] just traveling the state. Clinton did the best job I've ever seen of an individual sitting on a statewide organization."[86] All that traveling paid off; Clinton won both the primary and the general election.

Many people felt that the attorney general's job was just a stepping stone to the Arkansas governor's mansion for Clinton, and two years later he proved them right. In 1978, at age thirty-two, he was elected governor of Arkansas—the youngest governor in the United States.

Arkansas Governor

Clinton launched many new and innovative programs during his first two-year term as governor, including a plan to reform Arkansas schools and establish an energy department. Yet in 1980 Clinton's political career was abruptly halted when he lost his re-election bid to a relatively unknown Republican opponent named Frank White.

There were many theories about why Clinton lost. Some blamed a huge increase in state motor vehicle fees, which were used to pay for new roads. Others pointed to a controversial plan for consolidating school districts. However, another point of view laid blame for the defeat squarely on Clinton. The feeling was that he had simply become too smug, thinking that only he and his young, progressive staff had the answers to Arkansas's problems.

"He didn't listen to anybody," veteran Arkansas legislator Lloyd George recalled of Clinton's first term as governor. "You couldn't tell

Bill Clinton as governor of Arkansas in 1988.

him anything. You couldn't talk to him. His people wouldn't even let his constituents see [him]."[87]

Though pained by his defeat, Clinton ultimately benefited from the loss. "Bill Clinton wouldn't be president today if he hadn't gotten beat for a second term," said George. "He was too arrogant and he thought he knew all the answers."[88]

Almost immediately after his defeat, Clinton began planning to run for governor against White in 1982. Demonstrating that he had learned from his mistakes, Clinton eagerly solicited advice from state lawmakers and veteran politicians. According to George, "He came back [to politics] a changed man."[89]

But others feel that not all of the changes in Clinton were good. The defeat, they say, made him cautious, unwilling to fight for ideas and programs unless opinion polls clearly showed that the public also supported them. "He went from hubris to never brushing his teeth without reading a poll,"[90] said a reporter who covered Clinton frequently.

When Clinton beat White in November 1982, he became the first governor in Arkansas history to win back the office after having been defeated. During his second term Clinton seemed less willing to push new, controversial ideas. When he did introduce new programs, he chose them carefully—promoting only those programs he knew had public support. By this time, according to political consultant Ernest Oakleaf, Clinton may have already been considering a run for the presidency, which would explain his new, cautious approach. "I always felt that from then on [after being re-elected as governor] his eye was on the bigger prize and that he was very cautious and would do whatever it took to stay in office,"[91] recalled Oakleaf.

An Unexpected Announcement

Clinton was re-elected governor of Arkansas twice more, in 1984 and 1986. By now he was becoming a national political figure—one of the new breed of Democrats who were not wedded to the party's traditional support for government social programs. Many political observers thought that Clinton would run for the Democratic nomination for president in 1988. It seemed like an opportune time: The incumbent Republican president, Ronald Reagan, could not run for another term; the Republican Party and its likely nominee, Vice President George Bush, seemed to be vulnerable; and, there was no dominant Democratic candidate.

All signs in the Clinton camp seemed to point toward "Go" for a presidential run. But in July 1987 Clinton stunned his supporters by announcing that he would not be a candidate in 1988. He said that the rigors of a campaign would keep him away too long from his daughter Chelsea, who was just seven years old. Some people accepted this explanation. Others, however, felt that different concerns kept him out of the race. Chief among these was a rumor of marital difficulties between the Clintons, prompted by reports of infidelity by the governor. As one veteran reporter remembers, "There was a lot of speculation about why he didn't run. I was very curious about that too. The rumors of womanizing were afoot and a lot of people thought that he was afraid of it all blowing up in his face at that point."[92]

Although he did not run for president, Clinton remained in the national political spotlight. Sometimes, though, the attention that he received was not the type he wanted. For instance, in July 1988 he gave a long, rambling speech at the Democratic National Convention. Because of its verbosity, the speech became prime political fodder for friends and foes alike. A few days later, however, he rebounded, demonstrating the remarkable capacity to bounce back from mishaps that has marked his political career. In an appearance on the *Tonight Show with Johnny Carson*, Clinton ridiculed his own speech and won over the studio audience with his ability to laugh at himself. He even played his saxophone with the studio orchestra.

Clinton continued to maintain a high political profile. In 1989 President George Bush named Clinton as cochairman of a national governors meeting on improving education. In 1990 Clinton won his fifth term as Arkansas governor and was also appointed chairman of the Democratic Leadership Council, a group that was exploring ways for the party to regain the presidency.

The Run for the White House

Deciding that the time had finally come for a shot at the White House, on October 3, 1991, Clinton announced his candidacy for the presidency. It did not take long for rumors of his extramarital affairs to resurface. The rumors took on a name and a face in January 1992, when a woman named Gennifer Flowers publicly claimed to have had an affair with Clinton. The resulting barrage of negative publicity threatened to not only destroy Clinton's chances to win the vital New Hampshire presidential primary in February but also to sink his candidacy.

Swiftly the Clinton camp moved to minimize the damage. Clinton and his wife, Hillary, went on national television and admitted that there had been trouble in their marriage but that they were working to repair it. The governor, however, denied having had an affair with Flowers. Although the Clinton campaign was temporarily rattled by the adultery charge, it recovered. By the end of January, polls showed Clinton leading other Democratic presidential contenders in New Hampshire.

But then another controversy erupted. Questions arose over Clinton's draft deferment during the Vietnam War. Although he never totally silenced the charge that he was a draft dodger, Clinton did deflect some of the criticism. He pointed out that he had exposed himself to the military lottery system by not entering the ROTC and might well have been drafted after all.

Although failing to regain all of the ground he had lost, Clinton finished a strong second in the New Hampshire primary with 26 percent

During the 1992 presidential campaign Gennifer Flowers publicly announced that she had an affair with Bill Clinton.

of the vote. (The winner, former Massachusetts senator Paul Tsongas, received 34 percent.) Clinton knew that he was fortunate to still be in the race at all; scandals such as those that had struck his campaign had destroyed other politicians in the past.

Yet Clinton had managed not only to survive but also to record an extremely credible showing. In recognition of his strong second-place finish in New Hampshire, Clinton threw a party, during which he proclaimed himself "the Comeback Kid." The name stuck, and Clinton used it throughout the rest of the primaries. By the time of the Democratic National Convention he was the overwhelming favorite for the presidential nomination. In July 1992 the Democrats nominated Clinton and Tennessee senator Al Gore for president and vice president.

Clinton's Republican opponent in the general election was incumbent president George Bush. Bush, a decorated World War II naval aviator who had a long, stable marriage, repeatedly questioned Clinton's character, emphasizing the reports of womanizing and draft dodging. There were so many allegations and rumors circulating about Clinton that members of his staff created a "Scandal Control Unit." It had the job of responding to the rumors as they arose, before they could damage the campaign.

As he had done throughout his political career, Clinton survived all of the scandals and rumors to claim victory in yet another election. Clinton defeated Bush in November 1992 by a substantial margin. He carried 32 states with 370 electoral votes to Bush's 18 states and 168 electoral votes. A third-party candidate, H. Ross Perot, did not win a single state.

A New Era Starts Off Badly

Many people felt that the election of Clinton and Gore signified a new era in American politics. Clinton was the first U.S. president born after World War II, and both he and Gore seemed to be the type of young, vigorous leaders that America needed as the twenty-first century approached.

The Clinton administration got off to a poor start, however, making one blunder after another. Clinton's first two nominees for attorney general had to be dropped at the last minute when it was revealed that each had employed illegal aliens.

After the uproar over the two failed attorney general appointments, and several other incidents that occurred during his first few months in office, Clinton was anxious to put controversy behind him and get on with the business of running the country. However, another problem cropped up on May 19, 1993, when seven career employees from the White House Travel Office were abruptly fired. Reports surfaced indicating that people close to the Clintons, who wanted a piece of the travel business for themselves, had instigated the job terminations. It was further alleged that White House staffers had asked the FBI to investigate the employees, thus raising concerns that the administration had improperly used the FBI to justify the firings.

The Clinton administration came under intense criticism for the seemingly partisan manner in which the Travel Office terminations were handled. After a few days the White House said that the employees had been placed on administrative leave and that five had been given new jobs. Two months later the White House admitted that some staffers had acted inappropriately in firing the workers. Clinton eventually apologized for the tawdry way the entire affair had been handled.

Yet another scandal broke when it was revealed that the White House personnel security office had requested approximately seven hundred confidential FBI background files. Included among these were files on prominent Republicans such as former secretary of state James Baker and former national security adviser Brent Scowcroft, both of whom had served under George Bush. Clinton staffers said they had requested the files to update White House security records. Administration opponents, however, charged that the White House was trying to dig up dirt on prominent Republicans. Clinton downplayed the entire incident, calling it just a bureaucratic error.

The Whitewater Investigation

Although these scandals put the Clinton administration in a bad light, they had no serious consequences or lasting effects. This was not the case with the next series of scandals. These events would eventually lead to the impeachment of an American president for only the second time in U.S. history.

The complicated scandal began in the autumn of 1993 over a failed land development deal, known as Whitewater, which the Clintons had been involved in years before in Arkansas. Some friends of the Clintons, as well as Hillary Clinton's law firm, were also involved in Whitewater, and questions were being raised about whether the Clintons had been engaged in any illegal activity in connection with the venture.

News about Whitewater began dominating the Clinton presidency despite the fact that both the president and his wife consistently denied any wrongdoing. "I can't give a press conference without being asked about this," a frustrated Clinton said at one point. "I can't take this."[93] Hoping to calm the storm of allegations and push the scandal off the front pages, the president asked that an independent counsel be appointed to investigate Whitewater. In January 1994 Attorney General Janet Reno named an independent counsel, who served only briefly; Kenneth Starr succeeded him in the summer of 1994.

For several years Starr pursued the Whitewater investigation. Although he uncovered enough evidence of criminal activity to bring fraud charges against several associates of the Clintons, he was unable to find evidence against either the president or his wife.

The Paula Jones Case

This, however, did not mean that the president was in the clear. At approximately the same time that the Whitewater investigation

Paula Jones (left) accused Clinton of making sexual advances to her while he was governor of Arkansas in 1991.

began, yet another scandal was brewing over one of Clinton's alleged extramarital sexual encounters. This one concerned a woman named Paula Jones, who claimed that Clinton had made a sexual advance (which she had refused) in May 1991, when he was still governor of Arkansas. After the story became public, Jones felt that she needed to protect her reputation. Although she initially wanted only an apology from the president, Clinton's refusal to acknowledge ever meeting her prompted her to file a seven-hundred-thousand-dollar sexual harassment suit against him. At this time, the Jones lawsuit was following a separate track from the Whitewater investigation. That would not be the case in the future, however.

Despite Whitewater and other allegations of scandal during Clinton's first term, the Democrats renominated the president for a second term in 1996. In the general election Clinton swept past Republican Robert Dole to victory, becoming the first Democratic president since Franklin D. Roosevelt to win two terms.

The Scandals Merge

Clinton's triumph was short-lived, however. The lawyers for Paula Jones had learned that a young woman named Monica Lewinsky had had an affair with the president while working as a White House intern. Soon there were indications that the president might have been guilty of lying under oath, tampering with a witness, and obstructing justice. Jones's lawyers told Starr about these developments, and the independent counsel asked and received from Attorney General Reno authority to investigate the Lewinsky matter as well as Whitewater.

When the Lewinsky situation was first publicly reported early in 1998, Clinton emphatically denied any involvement with her. "I want to say one thing to the American people. I did not have sexual relations with that woman, Miss Lewinsky," said the president on January 26, 1998, scowling and wagging his finger at television cameras. "I never told anybody to lie, not a single time—never. These allegations are false."[94]

By August, however, Clinton admitted that he had indeed had a relationship with Lewinsky that was "not appropriate" and "wrong." "I misled people, including even my wife," he said to a national television audience. "I deeply regret that."[95]

Impeachment

On September 9, 1998, Starr sent to the U.S. House of Representatives 450 pages of material that he believed constituted grounds for

Monica Lewinsky testified about her relationship with President Clinton in a videotaped deposition during his impeachment trial in the Senate.

Clinton's impeachment. Starr's report cited eleven possibly impeachable offenses allegedly committed by the president. After examining the evidence, the House Judiciary Committee voted on December 11 and 12 to send four articles of impeachment to the full House of Representatives. The president was charged with perjury before a grand jury, perjury in a deposition given in the Paula Jones case, obstruction of justice, and abuse of power.

On December 19 the House impeached Clinton by approving two articles: those charging perjury before a grand jury and obstruction of justice. Thus, Clinton became the first elected president ever to be impeached. (Andrew Johnson, the other impeached president, had been Abraham Lincoln's vice president, and had assumed office after Lincoln's assassination.)

For an impeached official to be removed from office, the U.S. Constitution requires approval of one or more of the articles of impeachment by a two-thirds majority of senators (sixty-seven in 1999). On February 12, 1999, in a historic vote with all one hundred senators present, the Senate rejected both articles. The first article, dealing with perjury, received just forty-five "yes" votes. The second article, concerning obstruction of justice, tallied fifty "yes" votes.

After the Senate vote, the president appeared in the White House Rose Garden and apologized to the nation. "I want to say again to the American people how profoundly sorry I am for what I said and did to trigger these events,"[96] he said. While the Senate vote ended the Lewinsky matter, the Whitewater investigation remained ongoing. As of the fall of 2000, no charges had been filed against either of the Clintons in the Whitewater affair.

Establishing a Legacy

With impeachment behind him, Clinton sought to conclude his presidency on a positive note. He continued his efforts at promoting peace in Northern Ireland, the Middle East, and elsewhere, and he took strong positions on important domestic issues, such as advocating greater gun control and more environmental preservation. Through these actions, it seemed Clinton was trying to establish a legacy as far removed from impeachment as possible.

Clinton has tried to downplay the significance of his impeachment. "I do not regard this impeachment vote as some great badge of shame,"[97] he said in March 1999. Yet despite his hopes and deeds, Clinton's presidency will likely be measured by his impeachment, just as Watergate dominates the Nixon years and Teapot Dome defines Harding's term. History has a long memory when it comes to presidential scandals.

NOTES

Chapter 1: Presidential Scandals in Perspective

1. Quoted in John Bartlett, *Familiar Quotations*. Boston: Little, Brown, 1980, p. 615.

2. Quoted in Hope Ridings Miller, *Scandals in the Highest Office*. New York: Random House, 1973, p. 46.

3. Quoted in Miller, *Scandals in the Highest Office*, p. 66.

4. Quoted in Shelley Ross, *Fall from Grace*. New York: Ballantine Books, 1988, p. 62.

5. Quoted in Ross, *Fall from Grace*, p. 95.

6. Quoted in Ross, *Fall from Grace*, p. 94.

7. Quoted in Ross, *Fall from Grace*, p. 254.

8. Quoted in Ross, *Fall from Grace*, p. 82.

9. Quoted in Ross, *Fall from Grace*, p. 91.

10. Quoted in Miller, *Scandals in the Highest Office*, p. 66.

11. Quoted in Miller, *Scandals in the Highest Office*, p. 66.

12. Quoted in Miller, *Scandals in the Highest Office*, p. 67.

Chapter 2: Ulysses S. Grant

13. Quoted in William S. McFeely, *Grant*. New York: W. W. Norton, 1981, p. 48.

14. McFeely, *Grant*, p. 48.

15. Quoted in McFeely, *Grant*, p. 51.

16. Quoted in McFeely, *Grant*, p. 52.

17. Quoted in McFeely, *Grant*, p. 60.

18. Quoted in McFeely, *Grant*, p. 64.

19. Quoted in McFeely, *Grant*, p. 73.

20. Quoted in McFeely, *Grant*, p. 101.

21. Quoted in Nancy Scott Anderson and Dwight Anderson, *The Generals: Ulysses S. Grant and Robert E. Lee*. New York: Alfred A. Knopf, 1988, p. 245.

22. Quoted in McFeely, *Grant*, p. 169.

23. Quoted in Bruce Catton, *The American Heritage Picture History of the Civil War*. New York: American Heritage/Bonanza Books, 1960, p. 500.

24. Quoted in McFeely, *Grant*, p. 277.

25. Quoted in McFeely, *Grant*, p. 408.

26. Quoted in Henry Graff, ed., *The Presidents*. New York: Charles Scribner's Sons, 1984, p. 306.

27. Quoted in McFeely, *Grant*, p. 493.

28. Quoted in McFeely, *Grant*, p. 516.

Chapter 3: Warren G. Harding

29. Quoted in Graff, *The Presidents*, p. 465.

30. Quoted in Francis Russell, *The Shadow of Blooming Grove*. New York: McGraw-Hill, 1968, p. 114.

31. Quoted in Russell, *The Shadow of Blooming Grove*, p. 94.

32. Russell, *The Shadow of Blooming Grove*, p. 159.

33. Quoted in Russell, *The Shadow of Blooming Grove*, p. 159.

34. Quoted in Andrew Sinclair, *The Available Man*. New York: Macmillan, 1965, p. 49.

35. Quoted in Russell, *The Shadow of Blooming Grove*, p. 252.

36. Quoted in Sinclair, *The Available Man*, p. 63.

37. Quoted in Russell, *The Shadow of Blooming Grove*, p. 216.

38. Quoted in Russell, *The Shadow of Blooming Grove*, p. 109.

39. Quoted in Russell, *The Shadow of Blooming Grove*, p. 341.

40. Quoted in Russell, *The Shadow of Blooming Grove*, p. 383.

41. Quoted in Graff, *The Presidents*, p. 468.

42. Quoted in Russell, *The Shadow of Blooming Grove*, p. 443.

43. Quoted in Russell, *The Shadow of Blooming Grove*, p. 453.

44. Quoted in Russell, *The Shadow of Blooming Grove*, p. 485.

45. Quoted in Russell, *The Shadow of Blooming Grove*, p. 463.

46. Quoted in Russell, *The Shadow of Blooming Grove*, p. 558.

47. Quoted in Russell, *The Shadow of Blooming Grove*, p. 559.

48. Quoted in Sinclair, *The Available Man*, p. 285.

49. Quoted in Russell, *The Shadow of Blooming Grove*, p. 588.

50. Quoted in Russell, *The Shadow of Blooming Grove*, p. 640.

Chapter 4: Richard M. Nixon

51. Quoted in Roger Morris, *Richard Milhous Nixon*. New York: Henry Holt, 1990, p. 84.

52. Quoted in Fawn M. Brodie, *Richard Nixon, the Shaping of His Character*. New York: W. W. Norton, 1981, p. 99.

53. Quoted in Morris, *Richard Milhous Nixon*, p. 273.

54. Quoted in Morris, *Richard Milhous Nixon*, p. 271.

55. Quoted in Morris, *Richard Milhous Nixon*, p. 319.

56. Quoted in Brodie, *Richard Nixon, the Shaping of His Character*, p. 171.

57. Quoted in Morris, *Richard Milhous Nixon*, p. 402.

58. Quoted in Brodie, *Richard Nixon, the Shaping of His Character*, p. 241.

59. Quoted in Brodie, *Richard Nixon, the Shaping of His Character*, p. 233.

60. Quoted in Morris, *Richard Milhous Nixon*, p. 619.

61. Quoted in Morris, *Richard Milhous Nixon*, p. 789.

62. Quoted in Morris, *Richard Milhous Nixon*, p. 831.

63. Quoted in Morris, *Richard Milhous Nixon*, p. 832.

64. Quoted in Brodie, *Richard Nixon, the Shaping of His Character*, p. 463.

65. Stephen E. Ambrose, *Nixon: Ruin and Recovery, 1973–1990*. New York: Simon & Schuster, 1991, p. 12.

66. Quoted in Ambrose, *Nixon*, p. 14.

67. Quoted in Ross, *Fall from Grace*, p. 226.

Chapter 5: Ronald Reagan

68. Quoted in Lou Cannon, *Reagan*. New York: G. P. Putnam's Sons, 1982, p. 26.

69. Quoted in Cannon, *Reagan*, p. 45.

70. Quoted in Cannon, *Reagan*, p. 97.

71. Quoted in Cannon, *Reagan*, p. 117.

72. Quoted in Cannon, *Reagan*, p. 223.

73. Quoted in Cannon, *Reagan*, p. 226.

74. Quoted in Cannon, *Reagan*, p. 304.

75. Quoted in Cannon, *Reagan*, p. 304.

76. Cannon, *Reagan*, pp. 306, 375.

77. Haynes Johnson, *Sleepwalking Through History*. New York: W. W. Norton, 1991, p. 50.

78. Johnson, *Sleepwalking Through History*, p. 169.

79. Quoted in Johnson, *Sleepwalking Through History*, p. 184.

80. Quoted in Bob Woodward, *Shadow*. New York: Simon & Schuster, 1999, p. 99.

81. Woodward, *Shadow*, p. 113.

82. Quoted in Woodward, *Shadow*, p. 128.

83. Quoted in Woodward, *Shadow*, p. 148.

84. Johnson, *Sleepwalking Through History*, p. 180.

Chapter 6: Bill Clinton

85. Quoted in David Gallen, *Bill Clinton as They Know Him*. New York: Gallen, 1994, p. 36.

86. Quoted in Gallen, *Bill Clinton as They Know Him*, p. 74.

87. Quoted in Gallen, *Bill Clinton as They Know Him*, p. 82.

88. Quoted in Gallen, *Bill Clinton as They Know Him*, p. 82.

89. Quoted in Gallen, *Bill Clinton as They Know Him*, p. 104.

90. Quoted in Gallen, *Bill Clinton as They Know Him*, p. 106.

91. Quoted in Gallen, *Bill Clinton as They Know Him*, p. 107.

92. Quoted in Gallen, *Bill Clinton as They Know Him*, p. 187.

93. Quoted in Woodward, *Shadow*, p. 237.

94. Quoted in Woodward, *Shadow*, p. 394.

95. Quoted in Woodward, *Shadow*, p. 444.

96. Quoted in Woodward, *Shadow*, p. 513.

97. Quoted in Woodward, *Shadow*, p. 516.

For Further Reading

Robert Cwiklik, *Bill Clinton: Our Forty-Second President.* Brookfield, CT: Millbrook, 1993. A good biography of Clinton up to his 1992 presidential victory.

John Devaney, *Ronald Reagan, President.* New York: Walker, 1990. This volume covers Reagan's life in detail.

Barbara Silberdick Feinberg, *American Political Scandals Past and Present.* New York: Franklin Watts, 1992. A look at many of the various scandals in American politics throughout history.

Martin S. Goldman, *Richard M. Nixon, the Complex President.* New York: Facts On File, 1998. A comprehensive biography of Nixon.

Elaine Landau, *Bill Clinton and His Presidency.* New York: Franklin Watts, 1997. A study of the first term of Clinton's presidency, including the controversies.

WORKS CONSULTED

Stephen E. Ambrose, *Nixon: Ruin and Recovery, 1973–1990*. New York: Simon & Schuster, 1991. An examination of the later part of Nixon's career.

Nancy Scott Anderson and Dwight Anderson, *The Generals: Ulysses S. Grant and Robert E. Lee*. New York: Alfred A. Knopf, 1988. A chronicle of the Civil War careers of both men.

Thomas A. Bailey, *Presidential Saints and Sinners*. New York: Free, 1981. A listing of presidents and the scandals that have befallen them.

John Bartlett, *Familiar Quotations*. Boston: Little, Brown, 1980. A book of famous statements by famous people.

Fawn M. Brodie, *Richard Nixon, the Shaping of His Character*. New York: W. W. Norton, 1981. A controversial look at the events that the author believes shaped Nixon's personality.

Michael Burlingame, *The Inner World of Abraham Lincoln*. Urbana: University of Illinois Press, 1994. A revealing look at some of the events in Lincoln's life that shaped his character.

Lou Cannon, *Reagan*. New York: G. P. Putnam's Sons, 1982. An excellent biography of Reagan up to the early years of his first administration.

Bruce Catton, *The American Heritage Picture History of the Civil War*. New York: American Heritage/Bonanza Books, 1960. A classic reference source on the Civil War.

David Gallen, *Bill Clinton as They Know Him*. New York: Gallen, 1994. A biography of Clinton, in the words of those who had contact with him, all the way up to his election as president.

Henry Graff, ed. *The Presidents*, New York: Charles Scribner's Sons, 1984. An excellent reference source on American presidents.

Haynes Johnson, *Sleepwalking Through History*. New York: W. W. Norton, 1991. An excellent though not unbiased account of American society during the Reagan era.

Robert E. Levin, *Bill Clinton: The Inside Story*. New York: S. P. I. Books, 1992. A chronology of Bill Clinton's career up until his election as president.

David Maraniss, *First in His Class*. New York: Simon & Schuster, 1995. A detailed biography of Bill Clinton up until he declared his candidacy for president in 1991.

William S. McFeely, *Grant*. New York: W. W. Norton, 1981. A comprehensive biography of Grant that is not afraid to express both admiration and criticism.

Hope Ridings Miller, *Scandals in the Highest Office*. New York: Random House, 1973. A book that separates fact from fiction in the history of presidential scandals.

Roger Morris, *Richard Milhous Nixon*. New York: Henry Holt, 1990. A comprehensive look at Nixon's early career.

Robert Payne, *The Corrupt Society*. New York: Praeger, 1975. An examination of the role of corruption and scandal throughout the history of civilization.

Shelley Ross, *Fall from Grace*. New York: Ballantine Books, 1988. An overview of scandals in American politics.

Francis Russell, *The Shadow of Blooming Grove*. New York: McGraw-Hill, 1968. The definitive work on Harding's life.

Andrew Sinclair, *The Available Man*. New York: Macmillan, 1965. A look at Harding's political career, with little personal detail.

Bob Woodward, *Shadow*. New York: Simon & Schuster, 1999. A comprehensive look at how Watergate has affected every president, from Ford through Clinton, by one of the men whose reporting was instrumental in revealing the story behind the Watergate break-in.

INDEX

PICTURE CREDITS

About the Author

Russell Roberts graduated from Rider University in Lawrenceville, New Jersey. A full-time freelance writer, he has published over 175 articles and short stories, and 9 nonfiction books: *Stolen: A History of Base Stealing, Down the Jersey Shore, Discover the Hidden New Jersey, All About Blue Crabs and How to Catch Them, Ten Days to a Sharper Memory, 101 Best Businesses to Start, Endangered Species, Ancient Egyptian Rulers,* and *Lincoln and the Abolition of Slavery.*

He currently resides in Bordentown, New Jersey, with his family and a lazy, diabolical, impish but cute cat named Rusti.